Carl

SECOND EDITION

Conflict in Indo China

IAN SUTHERLAND

Nelson

an International Thomson Publishing company ITP®

Melbourne • Albany, NY • Belmont, CA • Boston • Cincinnati • Johannesburg
London • Madrid • Mexico City • New York • Pacific Grove, CA
Scottsdale, AZ • Singapore • Tokyo • Toronto

Nelson ITP®
102 Dodds Street
South Melbourne 3205

Email nelsonitp@nelson.com.au
Website http://www.nelsonitp.com

Nelson ITP® ***an International Thomson Publishing company***

First published 1990
Second Edition 1993
10 9 8 7 6
05 04 03 02 01 00 99

National Library of Australia
Cataloguing-in-Publication data

Sutherland, Ian.
Conflict in Indo China.
Bibliography.
Includes index.
ISBN 0 17 008845 6
1. Indochina — History. 2. France — Foreign relations — Indochina. 3. Indochina — Foreign relations — France. 4. United States — Foreign relations — Indochina. 5. Indochina — Foreign relations — United States. I. Title.
959

Designed by R.T.J. Klinkhamer
Cover designed by Elspeth Lacey
Cover photographs courtesy Scope Features/Rainer Straebe (front right), Austral-International (from left) and Ian Sutherland (back).
Typeset in 10/13 Trump Medieval by Post Typesetters
Printed in China by L. Rex Printing Co. Ltd.

Nelson Australia Pty Limited ACN 058 280 149 (incorporated in Victoria) trading as Nelson ITP.

CONTENTS

INTRODUCTION

FEATURES OF THIS BOOK

TO GAIN THE MOST VALUE out of studying Indo China, students should keep up to date with current events. Keep a folder to collect any interesting newspaper articles. Set aside a videotape to record any relevant news item, current affairs program or documentary. Keep any useful articles in magazines such as *Time*, the *Bulletin* or *Asiaweek*.

The questions/exercises in this book are designed to assist students to build up a good summary of the topic, and to encourage discussion and thinking. As well as the specific questions that relate to the material immediately preceding them, different types of questions and exercises to assist this process are also included:

Review: Answers should be fairly brief, to build a summary of the topic.

Discuss: In some cases students will need to do some further reading to allow full discussion. (Written answers may be required by some teachers.)

Research: These are to build up a deeper understanding of an issue.

Update: These are to direct the students to think of the current ramifications of some past events.

Structured questions: These may overlap with some other category of question or exercise, but are designed to provide an integrated understanding of a whole chapter.

Focus questions: These direct the students to particular issues in the material that follows.

Other features of the book are:

Document studies: These should be seen as extension exercises, to develop further understanding of some crucial issues, and skills in analysing relevant primary sources.

Biographical studies: These provide extended information on key characters.

Key events: Some chapters have a list of key events at the end, whilst others have a question designed to build up such a list. Students can develop their own list for chapters that have neither.

INDO CHINA PROFILE

	Vietnam	*Laos*	*Cambodia*
THE PEOPLE			
Population	70 m	4.3 m	8.6 m
Annual growth	2.2%	2.8%	2.2%
Ethnic groups	Vietnamese (85% +), Chinese, Cham, Khmer, Muong	Lao (50%) Laotheung, Hmong, tribal Thai	Khmer (90%), Chinese, Vietnamese
Religions	Buddhism, Cao Dai, Christian, Islam	Buddhism	Buddhism, Islam
Languages	Vietnamese (official), French, Chinese, Khmer, English	Lao (official), French	Khmer
THE COUNTRY			
Area	330 000 sq km	236 000 sq km	181 000 sq km
Capital (population)	Hanoi (3.1 m)	Vientiane (160 000 est.)	Phnom Penh (1 m est.)
Terrain	Coastal deltas, mountainous	Rugged mountains, plateaus	Large central plain, mountains in south-west and north
Climate	Tropical monsoon, cooler in north	Tropical monsoon	Tropical monsoon wet season June–Oct.

ACRONYMS

AATTV Australian Army Training Team Vietnam ('The Team').
APC Armoured Personnel Carrier.
ARVN Army of the Republic of Vietnam (South).
ATF Australian Task Force.
CIA Central Intelligence Agency (United States). Heavily involved in South Vietnam. Implicated in Diem's assassination.
COSVN Central Office for South Vietnam (Communist co-ordinating body).
DMZ Demilitarised Zone. The strip of land along the 17th parallel that was the border between North and South from 1954 to 1975.

DRV	Democratic Republic of Vietnam (North).
ICP	Indo-Chinese Communist Party.
MACV	Military Assistance Command, Vietnam. US military co-ordinating body.
NLF	National Liberation Front.
NVA	Army of North Vietnam. Also PAVN (People's Army of Vietnam).
OSS	Office of Strategic Services. Forerunner of the CIA.
PRP	People's Revolutionary Party. South Vietnamese Communist Party.
RVN	Republic of Vietnam (South).
VNQDD	Vietnamese Nationalist Party. Formed in 1927, largely destroyed by the French in 1930.

THE LANGUAGE OF WAR

APC	Armoured Personnel Carrier.
RPG	Rocket Propelled Grenade.
Charlie	Viet Cong soldier (VC = Victor Charlie).
Grunt	US Infantry soldier.
M-16	Standard US semi-automatic rifle. It had to be kept very clean to operate, and this was difficult in the jungle.
AK-47	Soviet-made rifle used by the NVA and the Viet Cong. Not as accurate as the M-16, but more reliable.
Ghosts	Name given by the grunts to the VC at night.
Fragging	Killing an officer, often with a fragmentation grenade.
Spooky (Puff the Magic Dragon)	Slow flying DC3 aircraft used by the US. Could fire 6000 rounds a minute.
Huey	American UH-1 helicopters.
Free Fire Zones	Designated areas where the Americans were free to shoot at anything that moved.

THE MAIN CHARACTERS

The French

Paul Doumer Colonial Governor, 1897–1902. Turned Indo China into a profitable exercise for the French.

Colonel de Castries French Commander at Dien Bien Phu.

Pierre Mendès-France Prime Minister during the Geneva Conference. He had opposed France's involvement from 1950.

The Vietnamese

Gia Long Head of the Nguyen Dynasty, he became Emperor of unified Vietnam in 1802.

Bao Dai Became the last Emperor of Vietnam in 1925. Forced out in 1955, he now lives in France.

Ho Chi Minh Founded the Indo-Chinese Communist Party and the Viet Minh. Led the fight against the French. President of the Democratic Republic of Vietnam from 1954 until he died in 1969.

Ngo Dinh Diem Returned to Vietnam as Prime Minister of South Vietnam in 1954. Murdered by army officers in 1963.

Ngo Dinh Nhu Corrupt and hated younger brother of Diem. Also assassinated.

Madame Nhu Nhu's wife — the Imelda Marcos of Vietnam.

Thich Quan Duc First of the Buddhist priests to set himself alight.

Duong Van ('Big') Minh Led the coup against Diem. Became President in April 1975 when Thieu fled, and he surrendered to the Communists.

Nguyen Khanh Prime Minister of South Vietnam during 1964.

Nguyen Cao Ky Air Vice Marshall. Prime Minister 1965–1966.

Nguyen Van Thieu President of South Vietnam from 1967 to April 1975. He became increasingly corrupt and ineffectual.

Le Duc Tho North Vietnamese negotiator at the Paris Peace Conference.

Van Tien Dung Led the final Communist offensive in 1975.

The Cambodians/Laotians

Norodom Sihanouk Appointed King of Cambodia in 1941, but later became Prime Minister until his overthrow in 1970. Co-operated with the Khmer Rouge until they arrested him in 1976. Led a resistance group against the Vietnamese occupation of Cambodia from 1982. Returned to Cambodia in 1990 as head of state during the UN transition period.

Lon Nol Led the coup against Sihanouk in 1970. Prime Minister until 1975.

Pol Pot Khmer Rouge leader.

Hun Sen From 1984, Vietnamese-supported leader of Cambodia.

Prince Souvanna Phouma Prime Minister of Laos from 1962 until the Communist Pathet Lao took over in 1975.

The Americans

Presidents

Harry Truman 1945–1953
Dwight Eisenhower 1953–1961
John F. Kennedy 1961–1963
Lyndon Johnson 1963–1969
Richard Nixon 1969–1974
Gerald Ford 1974–1977

Ambassadors to South Vietnam

Henry Cabot Lodge 1963–1964
Maxwell Taylor 1964–1965
Henry Cabot Lodge 1965–1967
Ellsworth Bunker 1967–1973
Graham Martin 1973–1975

Others

General William Westmoreland American Military Commander in Vietnam, 1964–1968.
Henry Kissinger Nixon's special negotiator at the Paris peace talks, 1969–1973. Then became Secretary of State until 1977.
Robert McNamara Secretary of Defense 1961 until his resignation in 1968. Changed from a 'hawk' to a 'dove'.
Daniel Ellsberg Responsible for having the Pentagon Papers published in 1971.

Australian Prime Ministers

Robert Menzies 1949–1966
Harold Holt 1966–1967
John Gorton 1968–1971
William McMahon 1971–1972
Gough Whitlam 1972–1975

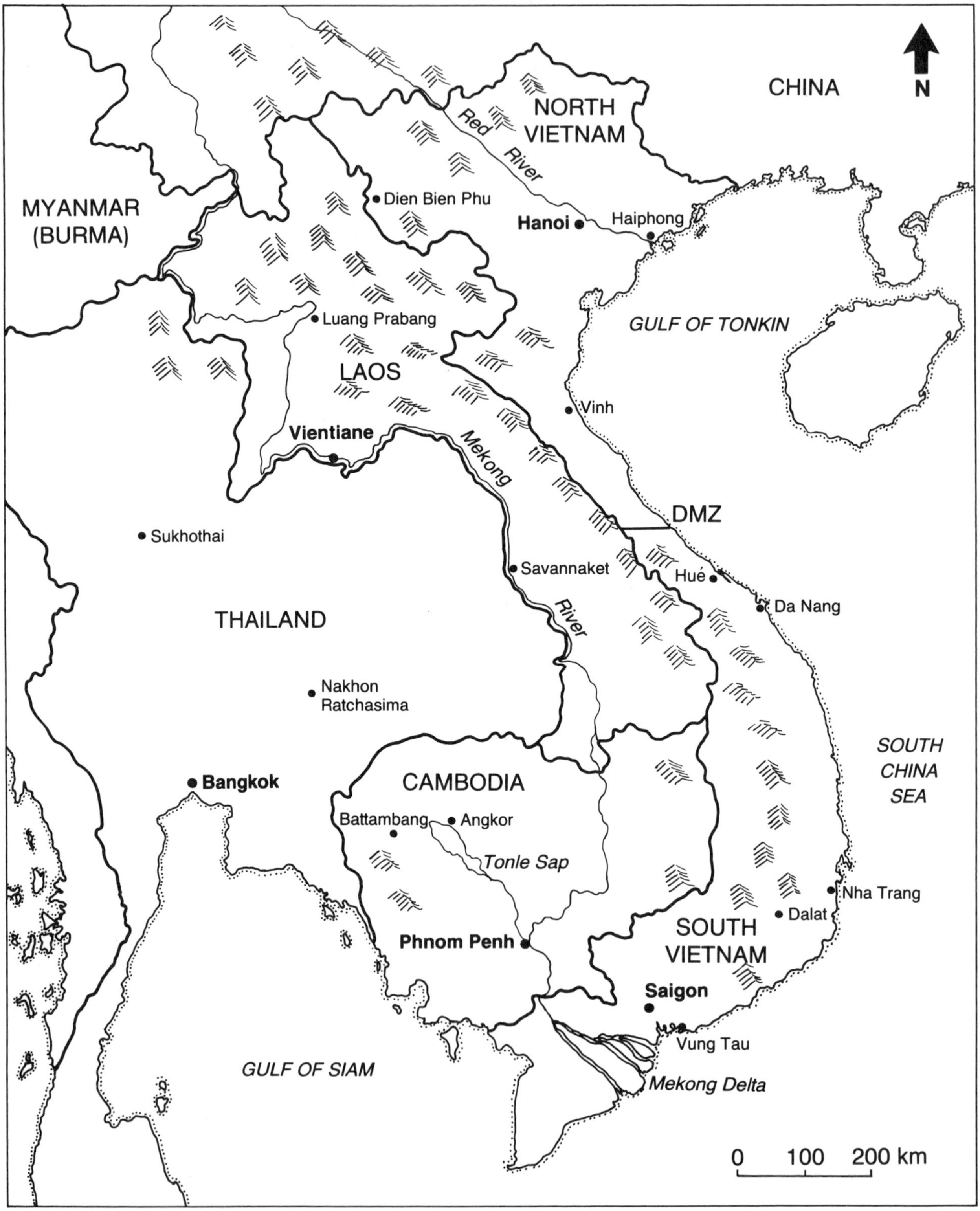
CHINA
N
NORTH VIETNAM
Red River
MYANMAR (BURMA)
Dien Bien Phu
Hanoi
Haiphong
Luang Prabang
GULF OF TONKIN
LAOS
Vinh
Vientiane
Mekong
DMZ
Sukhothai
Savannaket
Hué
Da Nang
River
THAILAND
Nakhon Ratchasima
SOUTH CHINA SEA
Bangkok
CAMBODIA
Battambang
Angkor
Tonle Sap
Nha Trang
Dalat
SOUTH VIETNAM
Phnom Penh
Saigon
Vung Tau
GULF OF SIAM
Mekong Delta
0 100 200 km

ISSUES

CHAPTER ONE

WHY STUDY INDO CHINA?

FOR MOST STUDENTS, the Vietnam War clearly shows up the generation gap between them and their parents. It was part of growing up for their parents' generation, and many were directly affected by it. Students see the war as a part of history, made more interesting because it has inspired so many films and because of its association with the supposedly 'Swinging Sixties'. The younger generation's view of the war is greatly distorted by this media view. Although the United States lost the war, many of the films are reluctant to recognise this, or to see the Vietnamese as real people. Richard Broinowski, Australia's ambassador to Vietnam from 1983 to 1985, has pointed out the dangers in this:

> "The Vietnamese war in which Australian forces took part will continue to be distorted by inaccurate, popularised reconstructions that are produced by many Western publishing houses in general and the American film industry in particular... They make money, stir prejudices and allow the consumer to ignore the damage left behind in Indo-China. Hollywood is particularly culpable. In all the movies about the war I have seen — including 'Coming Home', 'The Deer Hunter', 'Apocalypse Now', 'Platoon' and those egregious Rambo movies, the focus is on how the war has damaged American combatants, their psyche, their pride, their health, their moral values and the problem these disturbances have created back home. If they are there at all, the Vietnamese are seen as stereotypes or cardboard cut outs (usually wearing the wrong-shaped sun helmets), a backdrop against which Americans can measure, usually in highly moral terms, their own actions. There is in these films, as there was during the war, little attempt to understand Vietnamese culture, what motivated them (either northerner or southerner), or to acknowledge the enormous destruction visited on their country."

Richard Broinowski also points out the need for people to develop an objective and knowledgeable view of the war.

The Vietnam War and Australia: The Macquarie University Conference (1987). Foreword by Richard Broinowski.

> " Only then will all sides be able to see clearly just how poverty-stricken and damaged are the countries of Indo-China, and how desperately they need an international effort of cooperation to repair the ravages of war. "

In studying the Indo China conflict, students have to be careful to be objective, and to look at all sides of the issue. No statement should be accepted unquestioningly. *Good Morning Vietnam*, one film that does present a more sympathetic view of the Vietnamese people, shows how the truth could be manipulated during the war.

Historical perspective

A modern world study such as this is a different form of history. We cannot investigate it with the same degree of objectivity that we can apply to events further back in the past, such as the Great War. It is, for many people today, still an emotional issue, much more so than events from, say, the nineteenth century. It is also history that is still happening, that can influence our view of the events, and that requires us to keep watch on current events. Conflict is still present today in parts of South East Asia, there are still refugees trying to leave their country, as well as former refugees trying to establish themselves in their new countries or re-establish themselves in their old country. Countries in Indo China affected by the conflict are still reconstructing their political and economic systems, and re-establishing relations with other countries. Another current issue resulting from the conflict is the after-effects of the use of chemicals like Agent Orange on those who fought in Indo China and those who live there today. All these matters concern and influence people today, and will continue to be important for some time, even though Australia is no longer directly involved in the conflict. By understanding the historical background of the conflict, we can better understand the issues that influence us today.

HISTORICAL ISSUES

Students should consider some of the main historical issues that have recurred throughout the history of Indo China:

- Why was a peasant-based movement able to defeat major Western powers?
- Was the conflict a civil war, a revolution or an invasion?
- Were the Viet Minh and the Viet Cong Communists or nationalists?
- Did the Vietnamese people really want a Communist government? Why didn't an alternative government that they could have supported emerge?
- Were Bao Dai, Ngo Dinh Diem, Marshall Ky, General Thieu and Lon Nol the most

suitable leaders for their countries? Why did they receive support from some foreign governments?

- Could the Americans have won the war?
- What would have happened if the Americans had not become involved?
- At what stages during the conflict would a settlement have been possible?
- How did the involvement of the French and the Americans influence the type of countries that developed after their withdrawal?
- Why were the Vietnamese people able to put up with so much hardship?

ISSUES IN CONTENTION TODAY

The effects of the conflict in Indo China are still being felt in Australia, the United States and, most significantly, the nations of Indo China. Students can gain some idea of the importance of the issues by looking closely at newspapers, magazines and television. Read carefully the following articles, which are typical of stories you will find in the newspapers. Collect other articles about the main issues affecting Indo China, and use them to answer the questions on pages 10–11.

KHMER ROUGE HOLD UN SOLDIERS

PHNOM PENH, Wed: The Khmer Rouge is holding 21 UN peace-keepers captive in central Cambodia, the UN said yesterday.

The 21 comprise four UN military observers — from France, the U.S., China and Senegal — 15 Indonesian soldiers and two Cambodian translaters.

The group is being held near the provincial capital of Kompong Thom, while the UN attempts to secure their release.

"The Khmer Rouge office here said they knew nothing about it, but they swiftly issued an order from Phnom Penh ordering their release," a UN spokesman said.

The local Khmer Rouge commander has not issued any demands for the release of the peace-keepers, and the UN does not consider them hostages, the spokesman said.

"They are being detained against their will," he said.

The first detentions were yesterday when a French and Chinese military observer set off from Kompong Thom to meet UN workers.

The *Border Mail*, 17 December, 1992, p. 6

CAMBODIAN WOMEN BREAK HUNGER STRIKE

THREE Cambodian women yesterday ended a hunger strike to stave off deportation, which had lasted almost three months.

The Federal Court has agreed to hear their appeals for refugee status.

The director of medical services at Sydney's Auburn hospital, Dr Shu Thye, said the women called off the hunger strike and were in a satisfactory condition.

"We are giving them more fluids and then we'll put them on to solids," Dr Thye said.

"They are weak, but now that they will be eating soon, they will be back to normal quickly."

An Immigration Department spokesman said the women's lawyer lodged an application to the Federal Court on Tuesday to review the Government's decision to send the women back to Cambodia.

The spokesman said the court set a hearing date for February, but it could be heard earlier.

"It will be up to the Federal Court to direct the department to re-examine their claims for refugee status," the spokesman said.

The women began their hunger strike after the Government early this year rejected their applications to stay in Australia.

They arrived off the West Australian coast on March 31, 1990, with a group of boat people seeking asylum.

The *Border Mail*, 28 November, 1992, p. 6

Some of the 500 Australian troops in Cambodia in 1992, a long way from home (courtesy Rob Elliott)

Impact of the conflict on the nations of Indo China

Cambodia

- How successful have attempts to find peace in Cambodia been?
- What problems still remain?
- What role have the following countries played in the search for peace in Cambodia: Australia, ASEAN nations, Japan?
- How successfully have Cambodian refugees been resettled?
- What is life like for the people of Cambodia?

Vietnam

- How is the war still affecting the lives of the Vietnamese people, and the social and economic development of their country?
- How has the war affected Vietnam's relations with Australia, the USA, China and the ASEAN nations?
- In what ways has the war influenced Vietnam's role in Cambodia and Laos since 1975? What other factors have been important?

- How important is Communism, and the Communist Party, in Vietnam today?

Laos

- To what extent has Laos been influenced by Vietnam since 1975?
- How successful has Laos been in recovering from the war?

Australia's relations with Indo China

- Why is Australia held in high regard by the nations of Indo China?
- In what ways is Australia helping to rebuild and develop these countries?
- What role has Australia played in the search for peace in Cambodia?
- What economic links have developed between Australia and Vietnam?
- Examine Australia's diplomatic relations with Vietnam.
- What has Australia done to help solve the refugee problem?

The United States' relations with Indo China

- To what extent has the attitude of the USA been influenced by its defeat in the war? Has it been trying to punish Vietnam for its victory?
- What economic and political relations now exist between the USA and Indo-Chinese nations?
- In what ways is Vietnam still an issue in US politics? Look at other issues such as the Gulf War and presidential elections.
- How has the USA influenced the attitudes of other countries, and of the United Nations, towards the countries of Indo China?

REFUGEES

Most of the refugees from Indo China between 1975 and 1978 were from Laos, either ethnic Laotians or Meo (Hmong) who had fought against the Communists. These people crossed the border into Thailand. The refugee situation in Indo China changed after 1978 as large numbers started fleeing to escape the Killing Fields of Kampuchea (Cambodia). These refugees mostly ended up in camps along the Thai border.

In March 1978 Vietnam decided to implement fully its socialist policies in the South. There was already resentment in the South at the domination by the North. Now private trade was banned and 'new economic zones' were set up to resettle many of the people in the cities. Conscription was stepped up as Vietnam prepared for war with the Khmer Rouge. More and more people began to leave, many of them ethnic Chinese who had largely been involved in trade and who were increasingly discriminated against in the new Vietnam. About 675 000 people left Vietnam up to mid-1979, about 70 per cent of them ethnic Chinese. Some of these Chinese crossed the border into China but most of the other refugees left in boats, hoping to reach Hong Kong, Malaysia or Thailand. An unknown number of these boats did not reach land. Despite

In 1992, over 300 000 refugees were returned to Cambodia from camps in Thailand. These returnees need all the patience they have acquired during their years in exile for the long train trip home (courtesy Rob Elliott)

the great risks of the journey and an increasingly uncertain reception, many refugees continued to leave during the 1980s, with the number of boat people from Vietnam reaching a new peak during early 1989.

Support from the international community, and improved living standards in Vietnam, have seen an end to boat people leaving Vietnam. The European Community has provided $30 million to help returning refugees re-establish themselves through loans and job training. This help is only available to refugees who left before October 1991. Despite this aid, over 50 000 refugees still remained in camps in Hong Kong in early 1993, with the British Government applying pressure to have them returned to Vietnam. Many people are still anxious to leave Vietnam, but these people are now being handled officially through the Orderly Departure Program. Applicants are interviewed in Ho Chi Minh City, and are placed on priority waiting lists by countries such as Australia which are willing to accept them as migrants.

The journey

All of the refugees who have managed to reach Australia have faced enormous problems, and all of them have made great personal sacrifices. They have faced the risk of being caught whilst escaping, of leaving behind family and friends, and of arriving in a strange country with nothing. The experiences of the typical refugee from the three countries have much in common.

From Laos: Most refugees escaped by boat across the Mekong River into Thailand, where they spent years in refugee camps. The Phongsavans (Chapter

13) were luckier than most of the Laotian refugees, as they managed to bring with them some wedding photos, and they only stayed in the refugee camp for 18 months.

From Cambodia: Typical refugees escaped from Cambodia between 1979 and 1982, crossed the dangerous border into Thailand, and spent a few years in refugee camps along the Thai border. They faced great problems in these camps while they waited for a country to accept them as refugees. Leng Diep was accepted for Australia, and settled in Canberra. In 1984, he applied for his aunt and her two children to come to Australia. However, in early 1985, he received the following letter about Heng Sothavy, his niece, aged 16.

“Dear brother and sister,

Heng Sothavy died on 17-2-85 at 10pm in the Khao-I-Dang hospital, the day the Thai military rounded up the 'illegal' refugees in the camp. On the night of 16-2-85, Kim Hong [the mother], Sothavy, Sothany, and Uncle's family went to stay at the EDC centre where Kim Hong worked, thinking the place would not be searched by the Thai soldiers. Unfortunately, at three o'clock in the morning, about 2,000 Thai soldiers entered the camp and went through all the sections raiding every house searching for people like us.

When the soldiers came in, Kim Hong and her family hid themselves in the empty metal water tank to avoid being seen. They stayed in the tank all morning until noon without any food or water.

As the day became hotter, Sothavy begged to be let out, but because the soldiers were still around and they were afraid of being captured, Sothavy must remain in the tank. When she later became unconscious, her mother was very frightened and decided to come out of the tank. Even then, Sothavy was not taken to the hospital straight away, not until after the Thai soldiers had cleared out... at about 6 o'clock in the evening.

At the hospital she was diagnosed as having suffered from severe dehydration and brain damage from which she died at about 10 o'clock that night.

No-one could imagine that it would end up in tragedy like this for Kim Hong's family.

Sothavy's body was cremated on 18-2-85, but as yet no proper funeral ceremony has been arranged for her because the situation in the Camp is still very tense and confused.

We are very desperate and at times think of returning to Phnom Penh and facing the consequences. Please tell us what you think we should do...”

Canberra Times, May 1985

From Vietnam: The great majority of Vietnamese refugees to Australia left Vietnam secretly by boat. Nguyen Tuyet escaped in 1984.

“We left from Can Tho at the Dai Ngai estuary. I had to get there before four in the afternoon. I was able to get aboard the big boat which took us safely out to sea. At the time we didn't have to pay off anyone or bribe the coastal patrols, we made a clandestine escape. Then at sea, we sailed for three days and two nights and arrived at Palau Bidong [Malaysia]. We made our passage when the sea was rough so there weren't any Thai fishing boats. Our boat was only small, about 11 metres long. We had 20 people on board so we had plenty of food but we were seasick from the rough seas. ”

Interview with Nguyen Tuyet,CEP Oral History Project, National Library of Australia

Many Vietnamese were not as fortunate as the 20 on Tuyet's boat, as their captain was an excellent sailor. The Malaysians thought that his navigation was so good that he must have been sent by the Communists.

“ Tens of thousands of refugees — perhaps 100 000, — died en route, many at the hands of pirates in the South China Sea and the waters of the Indonesian archipelago. One estimate by the United Nations High Commission for Refugees is that 35 per cent were either lost at sea or murdered by pirates. Another 30 per cent are believed to have been captured by Vietnamese authorities. Many are permanently scarred by the trip. Children watched their mothers being raped and their fathers murdered by pirates. Before that there had been suffering in their homelands — either in the 'Killing Fields' or the so-called re-education camps. Today, Vietnamese, Cambodians and Laotians are being counselled at a special centre for torture victims in Sydney's western suburbs. ”

Bill Mellor and Matthew Ricketson, *Time*, 8 April, 1991

Discuss

- In what ways were the experiences of refugees from the three countries similar? How were they different?
- Why didn't the refugees stay in Thailand, Malaysia or Indonesia?

Refugees in Australia

Nguyen Tuyet was excited when she was told that she had been accepted to Australia, and she celebrated by having a party and frying her instant noodle rations and sprinkling them with sugar. However, after two years in Australia she was unemployed and facing a different society.

“ There are customs which are very odd as far as we Vietnamese are concerned. For example, when I had only just arrived there was the business of closing all the doors and windows or closing up the shops. It was so weird. This is because in our Vietnamese society the doors of the houses are open, cafes and restaurants are all open. When guests arrive the doors are wide open to welcome them, while here if you are at home or have gone out the doors are all closed. It seems to be depressing and gloomy, living apart and separated. There appears to be no unity. ”

Interview with Nguyen Tuyet, CEP Oral History Project

Discuss

- What other aspects of life in Australia would people such as Tuyet find hard to adjust to?
- If you were suddenly forced to become a refugee and to flee to Vietnam, what aspects of life would you miss most?

> "The average Indochinese refugee family still lives in an overcrowded flat or a small house, the husband working in, perhaps, a car or softdrink factory; the wife a lowly paid piece worker in the garment industry; the parents unemployable because of their age and lack of English; the children, who may have missed years of schooling, struggling to master the language while at the same time attempting to keep up with a class in which most other pupils are native speakers. In such struggling families, tensions can run high. Children can become near-suicidal over their inability to fulfil their parents' expectations. Some find their way into street gangs that hang around the pinball parlours of predominantly Indochinese suburbs."

Bill Mellor and Matthew Ricketson, *Time*

Discuss

- What views of Indo-Chinese refugees do many Australians hold? Compare these views with the experiences of the refugees described above.
- Why do refugee parents have a high expectation of their children? What problems does this create?
- Collect newspaper and magazine stories about the Indo-Chinese in Australia. What view is given by the media?
- Many Indo-Chinese have achieved success in Australia. In what areas? In what other ways (social, cultural, economic, educational) have they contributed to Australia?

Immigration to Australia from South East Asia 1959-1990

Country	*No.*	*Country*	*No.*
Cambodia	17 660	Myanmar	7 870
China	45 850	Philippines	62 500
Hong Kong	46 160	Singapore	20 060
Indonesia	17 920	Sri Lanka	32 770
Japan	5 340	Thailand	7 710
Korea	12 560	Vietnam	119 490
Laos	9 400	Other	29 020
Malaysia	54 630		
		TOTAL ASIA	438 940
		TOTAL WORLD	3 537 000

Top 10 Source Countries of Birth

	1966–67			1991–92	
Country of birth	*No.*	*%*	*Country of birth*	*No.*	*%*
UK & Ireland	75 510	54.4	United Kingdom	14 465	13.5
Italy	12 890	9.3	Hong Kong	12 913	12.0
Greece	9 830	7.1	Vietnam	9 592	8.9
Yugoslavia	7 550	5.4	New Zealand	7 242	6.7
Germany	3 410	2.5	Philippines	5 917	5.5
New Zealand	2 750	2.0	India	5 608	5.2
USA	2 340	1.7	China	3 388	3.2
Netherlands	1 870	1.3	Taiwan	3 172	3.0
Lebanon	1 720	1.2	Malaysia	3 123	2.9
India	1 650	1.2	Sri Lanka	2 777	2.6
Sub Total	119 520	86.2	Sub Total	68 197	63.5
Other	19 160	13.8	Other	39 194	36.5
TOTAL	138 680	100.0	TOTAL	107 391	100.0

VIETNAM VETERANS

Fifty thousand Australians served in Vietnam, about one-third as conscripts; 500 were killed. The casualty rate is low when compared to World War II, but the effects on the soldiers who returned were in many ways more serious. Many aspects of the war combined to make it a uniquely stressful experience, and many of the symptoms of stress only emerged years afterwards. The soldiers spent long periods exposed to danger, supposedly protecting people whom they disliked and did not understand. They were taken by jet from Vietnam, usually arriving in Sydney at night to avoid protesters, and were not given a period to readjust to civilian life. The Australia they returned to was an alien place where Vietnam was a subject to be avoided.

For many Vietnam veterans, being home was as strange an experience as the homecoming trip. Their time in Vietnam had meant not only adjusting to a strange culture and people but also adapting to the reality of death around them and the threat of their own death. By contrast, the Australia they came home to was in a boom era, and enjoying the luxury of isolation from the trouble spots of the world, including Vietnam. The society in which they had grown up seemed more alien to many of them than the one from which they had come. For many, the task of picking up their lives was seemingly impossible. Family life was difficult, and the divorce rate for veterans has been very high. Alcoholism and suicide have also been reportedly higher than the norm. Many veterans report sleep disturbances, nightmares, and emotional outbursts.

Until the early 1980s, Vietnam veterans had to face their problems by themselves. The Returned Soldiers League (RSL) was just as embarrassed as the rest of the community about the defeat in Vietnam, and only about 25 per cent of Vietnam veterans joined the RSL. One veteran turned up at an

Sandy and Frank of the Vietnam Veterans Motorcycle Club talk to fellow veteran Fr Lewis Nyman at a Long Tan Memorial Service in 1991. The official Welcome Home Parade in Sydney in 1987 gave recognition to the role of the soldiers, and has led to many other functions such as this one. The healing process culminated in the unveiling of the Vietnam Memorial in Canberra in October 1992 (Border Mail)

Anzac Day march wearing his medals, only to be told by a World War II digger that *his* medals had been earned in a 'real' war.

The formation of the Vietnam Veterans Association of Australia in 1980, set up mainly to deal with the Agent Orange issue, gave the veterans their own organisation to push for social and political recognition and financial compensation. Public interest in Vietnam increased in the mid-1980s, largely stimulated by a number of books and films. In October 1987, a large number of veterans gathered in Sydney for a reunion and a march through the city. For many this was the welcome home march they were denied at the time, and has helped the healing process.

In October 1992, an official memorial to the soliders who fought in Vietnam was unveiled in Canberra. This unveiling brought the veterans together and proved to be another step in the healing process.

AGENT ORANGE

Agent Orange was the most common of the many chemical mixtures used in Vietnam for defoliation, and contained equal parts of 2,4,5-T and 2,4-D. It penetrates the waxy covering of plant leaves and is absorbed into the plant's system, eventually causing its death. Soldiers on patrol were in contact with this foliage, and would often take their drinking water from streams where it had been sprayed. Agent Blue was a different mixture, used to destroy rice fields overnight. Traces of the extreme carcinogen, dioxin, were present in 2,4,5-T. Soldiers were also exposed to other insecticides, including DDT, chlordane, dieldrin, malathion and diazinon, sprayed by RAAF helicopters at the Nui Dat base three times a week.

Graham Walker in Kenneth Maddock & Barry Wright (eds), *War: Australia and Vietnam*, Harper & Row, Sydney, 1987, p. 221

> "Veterans' exposure to Agent Orange, research suggested, might be responsible for three categories of disability. The first was cancer, especially of the soft tissue and of the blood (lymphoma); the second, abnormalities in offspring; and the third, Toxic Brain Disfunction."

The last produced symptoms similar to stress disorders: rage, depression, skin rashes, chronic stomach troubles, headaches, occasional blurred vision, and loss of libido.

Effect on Australian soliders

By 1980, veterans were starting to report many of these three categories of disability and started to search for help. They found the Department of Veterans Affairs unsympathetic and received no help from the RSL. The newly formed Vietnam Veterans Association tried to get information from the government on the effects of Agent Orange, but found that questions asked in Parliament on the issue were generally not treated seriously. The Liberal Party had been in power during the Vietnam years and was again in power. It did not want any embarrassing information about the war being released.

When the Hawke Government was elected in 1983, it was more sympathetic to the veterans' claims and a Royal Commission was set up to inquire into the possible effects of Agent Orange on Australian soldiers. The commission, relying heavily on evidence submitted by the Monsanto chemical company,[1] reported that there was insufficient evidence to prove that disabilities were caused by Agent Orange. However, it did find that the stress of war had contributed greatly to any psychological problems suffered by veterans and that this was sufficient to entitle them to Repatriation benefits.

Compensation

In the United States, a class legal action on behalf of veterans was successful and resulted in the seven chemical companies involved in supplying the chemicals used in Vietnam setting up a fund to assist veterans. This fund has grown to $250 million, with $5 million set aside to help those Australians who were affected.

In South Korea, compensation is to be paid to its soldiers who were affected by Agent Orange.

Effect on the Vietnamese

However, the major effect of Agent Orange continues to be on the land and the people of southern Vietnam where over 80 million litres were dropped during the war. The chemical was used to deny the Viet Cong cover along river banks and in the jungle, and was also used to destroy crops in areas sympathetic to the Communists. The chemicals, including the carcinogenic dioxin, have passed into the food chain. Birth defects remain at very high levels, and the crops in many areas are still affected. Eucalyptus trees have been used to help in regeneration, particularly along the river banks.[2]

Review

- What have been the main problems faced by veterans since their return?
- Contact your local Vietnam Veterans Association to find out why veterans have had to face these problems, and what help they are now receiving?

Research

- Investigate further the effects of Agent Orange on the Vietnamese people.

CHAPTER TWO

THE CHINESE AND THE FRENCH

THE TERM INDO CHINA refers to that part of Asia situated between China and India, and influenced by those two dominant civilisations. Unlike China, India has had no direct influence on Vietnam. However it has had an important indirect influence through the spread of Buddhism, which reached Vietnam via China shortly after the birth of Christ. Buddhism rapidly replaced the primitive spirit beliefs of Vietnam's inhabitants and became the religion of the peasant masses who made up over 90 per cent of the population.

The modern country of Vietnam emerged in 1802 when it was unified by the Emperor Gia Long, the founder of the last of the Vietnamese dynasties. This unification ended a particularly brutal civil war that had divided the country for 200 years. It also meant that, for the first time in history, the area that we now know as Vietnam was controlled by one ruler. Previous dynasties had been centred in the North, around the Red River, and only with Gia Long did control extend to the southern edge.

Despite this new unity, the main influences and trends in Vietnamese history — the presence of the Chinese, the social and economic importance of the village, and a continual experience of warfare — had been present for many years before 1802, and continued after it.

THE CHINESE INFLUENCE

Vietnamese today have a deep-seated distrust of their huge northern neighbour, China. The most recent military attack by China on Vietnam came in 1979; the first was 2250 years ago. From 111 BC to 939 AD, Vietnam was taken over by China and subjected to ten centuries of domination. Since their expulsion in 939 until the present, the Chinese cultural and diplomatic influence has been very strong. The various Vietnamese dynasties had to keep on the right side of China by sending regular gifts (tribute) to the Chinese emperor as recognition of his superiority.

Confucianism was introduced into Vietnam during its period of domination and was used by the Chinese as an effective way of controlling their citizens. It was also very useful to the Vietnamese emperors later on, as it helped them retain power by reminding the citizens of their place in society. Under Confucianism, society was strictly organised. Everyone knew their place in this society, and had obligations to those below them and duties to those above them; women had only duties. The emperor was obliged to look after his people, and the people had to pay their dues to the emperor. The emperor was said to have the Mandate of Heaven to govern the country, which meant he was approved by the gods as ruler. This made it very hard for ordinary people to oppose him.

Confucianism brought with it the mandarins, the emperor's officials who carried out the administration of the country. They were not very popular.

> "All the visitors were outraged by the oppressive authority and rapacity of the mandarins, who took what they wanted without payment, punished ordinary citizens on the merest whim, and appeared free from any restraint. Surprisingly, the most senior of them and, by common consent, the most obnoxious and ill behaved, were eunuchs. Corruption was universal, and there was nothing that could not be bought."

P. J. Honey, *Genesis of a Tragedy*

This meant that Vietnamese society developed into two distinct groups:

- a Confucian elite, which was the ruling class and Chinese influenced, and
- the peasant masses.

When the French arrived in Vietnam, they replaced the Confucian elite with a Catholic elite.

THE MARCH TO THE SOUTH

Warfare has been a constant theme in Vietnamese life, as many other races have fought for the rich coastal land of Vietnam. After the Chinese were finally expelled in 939 AD, the Chams, an aggressive Indonesian race who were mostly seagoing pirates, tried to expand from the Champa Kingdom in Central Vietnam into the Red River delta, but were kept out by the Vietnamese. The strong Khmers expanded their empire from Cambodia and took over South Vietnam. About 1200, the present Vietnam was made up of three main areas as shown in the left-hand map on page 22.

Over the next 600 years, the Vietnamese gradually pushed south, with settlers following their successful soldiers and taking over the villages. The Cham capital was captured in 1470, and by 1708 the last of the Chams and the Khmers had been defeated. The Vietnamese were in control of all of the southern provinces, but instead of fighting other races, they now turned on themselves in civil war. The Nguyen and Trinh families fought each other for fifty years from 1620, before dividing the country between them. Fighting began again

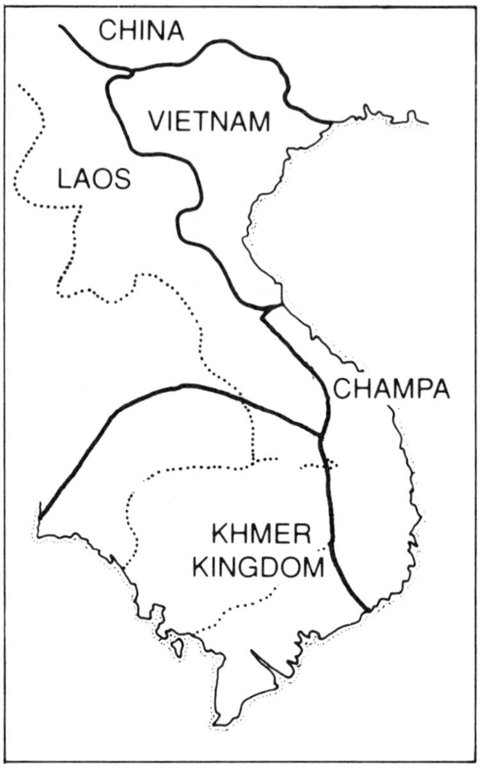

Left. *About 1200 AD the present Vietnam consisted of three main areas*

Right. *Indo China about 1700 AD*

in 1771 with the Tay Son Revolt, and lasted until the Nguyen dynasty, with some help from the French, defeated the Trinh in 1802. Vietnam was finally unified, with Nguyen Anh setting himself up as the Emperor Gia Long.

THE FRENCH ARRIVE

The first Europeans to arrive in Vietnam were Portuguese traders who landed in 1535. Merchants from other countries also tried to establish trade with Vietnam but with little success, and by 1700 all attempts had ceased. However, where the traders failed, the French Catholic missionaries had much greater success. The first missionaries started to spread the gospel in the 1630s, and by 1664 the Society of Foreign Missions was set up to carry on this work. The missionaries were backed by the (French) East India Company, which hoped that they might be able to open doors that had been closed to the traders. The French were right; many Vietnamese were receptive to Christianity, and by 1800 there were hundreds of thousands of converts.

The missionaries, frequently Jesuits, had a good political nose. One of them, Monsieur Pigneau de Béhaine, became involved in the civil war at the end of the eighteenth century on the side of the future Emperor Gia Long. He arranged for two ships and 400 soldiers to be made available. When Vietnam was unified in 1802 Gia Long was conscious of the debt that he owed to the missionaries, but he did not want to encourage the French. He tolerated Christianity, but made sure that the French were given no chance to extend their influence. His successors were under no obligation to the French missionaries, and in the 1830s started to persecute them and had ten of them executed.

This persecution did not stop the missionaries, who realised that a few martyrs would increase their popularity in France, and put more pressure on the government to back them up. One of them, Dominique Lefebvre, was twice expelled from Vietnam, but returned both times. The second time, in 1847, two warships were sent to help him. An incident at Hué led to the shelling of the city by the warships and hundreds of Vietnamese were killed. The French had arrived.

Poor government by the Nguyen emperors made it easier for the French to extend their influence. The Nguyen dynasty, founded in 1802 by Gia Long, was the most disastrous of all Vietnamese dynasties. The rulers were cruel, oppressive and ineffectual and opposition to the Nguyens increased during the nineteenth century. Local rebellions became common.

The French Emperor, Napoleon III, decided in the late 1850s to extend French influence in the area. In 1858, fourteen warships and 2500 soldiers were sent to Vietnam. Da Nang was taken easily, and the next year Saigon was attacked and its citadel destroyed. In 1861, the French claimed southern Vietnam (Cochin

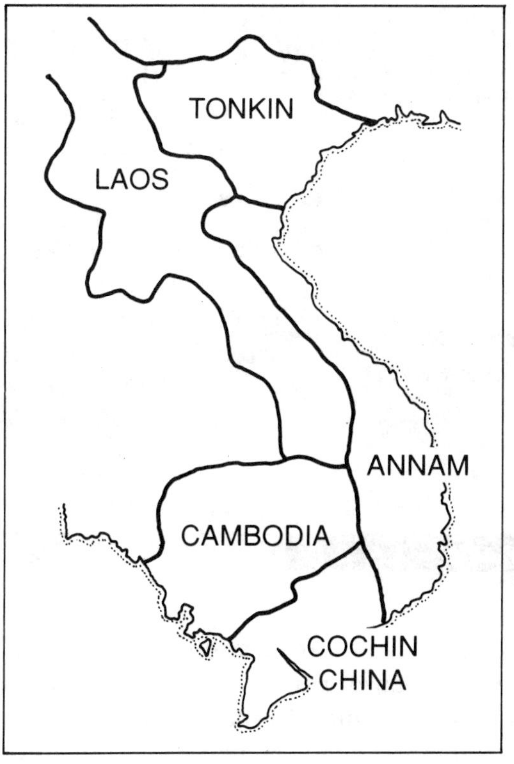

French Indo China

China) as a colony, and in 1862 forced the emperor to hand over three southern provinces.

Over the next twenty years the French gradually extended their control northwards. In 1885, the emperor was forced to sign the Treaty of Tientsin, handing over control of all of Vietnam to the French. The emperor kept his position, but the French were clearly in charge. Two years later they added Cambodia, and created the Indo-Chinese Union. Laos was added six years later, and the Union divided into five areas for administration: Cambodia, Laos, Tonkin (North Vietnam), Annam (Central Vietnam) and Cochin China (South Vietnam).

The French claimed to have interfered in the area to stop their missionaries being persecuted, but their real motives were to open the area for trade, and to back up their expansion into southern China.

> “Our compatriots, not well informed on history, suppose that France came to intervene in Annam solely for the protection of missionaries... The missionaries, in reality, have only been the pretext for our action against Annam. The loss of India in the eighteenth century, the increasingly rapid extension in the Far East of our perpetual rival England imposed on us the obligation to set foot in the China seas, the only alternative being our falling into a state of contemptible inferiority. Annam gave us the opportunity, the massacre of Frenchmen who were there as missionaries gave us the pretext.”

Captain Gosselin, French officer-historian, in 1904, in Robert Asprey, *War in the Shadows*, Macdonald & Janes, London, 1975, p. 596

Review

- Why would the Vietnamese distrust the Chinese?
- Outline the stages by which the French took over in Indo China. What were their motives?

Discuss

- Find out about Buddhism and Confucianism. How would they affect the lives of people in the villages in Vietnam?
- The first three Nguyen emperors were Gia Long, Minh Mang and Tu Doc. Why did they become so unpopular?

Update

- What place do Buddhism and Confucianism play in the Communist society of Vietnam today? Has there been any attempt to suppress them?

FRENCH RULE, 1886–1930

The French have long held a reputation as poor colonisers: repressive, racist and self-interested. Much of this reputation was earned in Indo China. Their general aim was to make Indo China pay for its own administration, and to encourage French companies and French settlers to move in and reap the profits.

Indo China was to be a source of raw materials for France, and a captive market for French manufacturers. These French interests were to be closely protected by the Security Service.

The Vietnamese were made to feel inferior in their own country. A leading Vietnamese nationalist wrote in 1906:

Joseph Buttinger, *Vietnam: A Dragon Embattled*, Phaidon Press, Oxford, 1967

> "Whether in newspapers, or letters, or conversation, the French always hold us in hatred and contempt. They consider us not merely as savages, but as dogs and swine. Not only do they not treat us as equals, but to them we are something dirty and stinking, to be avoided."

Land ownership

The vast majority of the Vietnamese people lived in villages and their main occupation was rice growing. This had been the pattern of their lives for centuries. All aspects of their lives were dominated by the village. It was the centre of their religious, cultural and economic lives and was also the most important administrative unit in Vietnam. The village authorities were responsible for the everyday running of the village, and during the many periods of conflict they were largely left alone by the central government.

French rule had a devastating effect on the Vietnamese people through changes to the method of land ownership. The French made grants of large areas of land to a few French settlers and to some Vietnamese who supported them. These grants were originally along the river plains of the North and later along the border areas.

This led to a very unequal land ownership system. It created a small class of rich and greedy landlords, who were either French or Vietnamese Catholics. The peasant masses were greatly exploited by their new landlords. Their rents could reach 60 per cent of their output for a year and they were forced to take loans at an average interest rate of 70 per cent. To this were added the land taxes imposed by the French, and the monopoly the French had on some basic items, such as salt, that pushed up prices.

Peasant problems were not new, but were made much worse by the French:

David Halberstam, *Ho*, Barrie & Jenkins, London, 1971, p. 7

> "It was a rotting society that was becoming increasingly ready for an upheaval. The arrival of the French simply postponed an inevitable revolution from within against the Mandarin class, and meant that when the revolution came, it was directed against the foreigners as well as against the upper class."

Economic effects

France had trouble in following a consistent policy in Indo China. For much of the time they ruled, the French were more concerned with their own problems of political instability, or World War I and its effects, than they were with running an empire. Up until 1926, there had been fifty-two different administrations in charge of colonial rule. The only person to make his mark was

Paul Doumer, who was colonial governor for five years up to 1902.

Doumer almost single-handedly changed Indo China from a financial loss into a profit-making enterprise for the French. He made the people pay for the cost of their own rule by increasing customs duties and direct taxes. He created official monopolies on salt, alcohol and opium. Doumer concentrated on building railways and lighthouses, whilst denying the people industrial development and education.

Education

Before French rule, about 80 per cent of the Vietnamese were roughly literate in Chinese characters. The French banned the Chinese system of writing and brought in *Quoc Ngu*, a modified alphabet system devised originally by a Frenchman and still in use today. It was a much simpler system, but was generally rejected by the Vietnamese because it was foreign. By 1940, only 20 per cent of boys, and a much smaller proportion of girls, were at school.

Only the wealthy few at the top of society had access to tertiary education, usually in France. When they returned, they were greatly disillusioned as they were rarely able to translate their educational qualifications into suitable employment opportunities. In France they were generally treated as equals, but on their return they were treated as inferiors by even the most minor French officials. The following two quotes give some idea of the situation.

Bernard Fall, *The Two Viet-nams: A Political and Military Analysis*, Frederick A. Praeger, New York, 1967

> “The French janitor at the University of Hanoi received a base pay that was slightly higher than that of a Vietnamese professor with a Ph.D. from the University of Paris.”

Halberstam, *Ho*, p. 11

> “It [education under the French] trained a generation of Vietnamese just enough to make them hunger for more, just enough to teach them the inequities of the system.”

Review

- What would be the main criticisms of French rule these people would make?
  (a) A student, just returned from university in France,
  (b) A worker on a rubber plantation,
  (c) A rice farmer in a small village.
- Draw up a time-line of the main events from 1802 to 1945.

Structured questions

- Briefly explain how France was able to gain control of Indo China.
- What did the French hope to gain?
- How was Vietnamese society affected by French rule up to 1930?

BAO DAI

The French were the real rulers of Vietnam, but they allowed emperors from the Nguyen dynasty to remain as their puppets. One of them, Emperor Duy Tan, proved difficult when he staged a revolt against French rule in 1916. He was rapidly exiled. In 1925, his grandson Bao Dai became emperor. Bao Dai had been raised and educated in France from the age of 9, and retained a fondness for the pleasures of French life. He did not return to Vietnam to take up his position until 1932. Helped by Ngo Dinh Diem, he made a token effort at ruling by himself before he accepted the reality of French rule. He then reached a mutually beneficial arrangement where the French allowed him to remain as their puppet emperor, and he allowed the French to pay the bills for his extravagant lifestyle. By 1952, this amounted to $4 million a year to cover a few houses and four private planes.

He remained as emperor during the years of Japanese occupation from 1940 to 1945, but resigned in 1945, handing his power over to Ho Chi Minh. The French persuaded him to make a return appearance as puppet emperor from 1949 to 1954, before he finally retired to live in France.

Stanley Karnow describes Bao Dai as 'a weak, unpredictable, corruptible playboy'. The writer, S. J. Perelman, met him in Hong Kong in 1946:

> "Bao Dai was seated in a snug alcove surrounded by several hostesses whose skinny necks and high-pitched avian cackle lent them more than a passing resemblance to a flock of spring fryers. The royal exile, a short, slippery-looking customer rather on the pudgy side and freshly dipped in Crisco, wore a fixed, oily grin that was vaguely reptilian."

Quoted in Stanley Karnow, *Vietnam: A History*, Penguin, 1986, pp. 172–3

Bao Dai, last Emporer of Vietnam (US Defense Department)

STIRRINGS OF NATIONALISM

CHAPTER THREE

1930–1946

THE VIETNAMESE never passively accepted French rule, and there were many outbreaks of violent resistance, all put down harshly by the French. The Japanese victory over Russia in 1905 showed what an Asian nation could do, and Japan became a centre for Vietnamese exiles. World War I gave impetus to this growth of nationalism; over 100 000 Vietnamese were forcibly recruited to serve in France, and many of them returned home with subversive ideas. President Wilson of the USA became a hero for them with his promises of freedom and self-determination for all peoples, not realising that he was generally referring to white races.

The early 1920s saw several attempts to establish moderate political parties in Vietnam. These parties got nowhere with the French and the Vietnamese quickly learned that moderation was pointless. This failure encouraged the growth of more radical, revolutionary groups. Two of these emerged by the late 1920s, both influenced by China: the VNQDD (Vietnamese Nationalist Party) and the ICP (Indo-Chinese Communist Party).

VIET NAM QUOC DAN DONG

The Viet Nam Quoc Dan Dong (VNQDD) was formed in 1927 with the aim of forcibly expelling the French from Vietnam. Its members had only a vague idea about the type of country they wanted to establish after they gained independence. The party tried to appeal to all Vietnamese, but was basically middle class and urban-oriented and strongest in the Hanoi area. By 1929, it had 1500 members, mostly teachers and government officials. Its terrorist activities, including assassination, attracted French attention and it was forced to launch a premature uprising in February 1930 before the French moved against it. This was a disaster, and the leaders were rounded up and executed.

The party survived for a few years, but was never again a threat to the French. The one nationalist group that might have been a serious rival to the Communists had been eliminated. The French thus made it easier for Ho Chi Minh to capture the support of the majority of Vietnamese, and harder for themselves later on to find any alternative to Ho and the Communists. These Communists shared with the VNQDD the belief that violence was necessary, but they had a very clear idea of the type of system they would develop once they were in power.

INDO-CHINESE COMMUNIST PARTY

In 1925, Ho Chi Minh was working in Canton as an interpreter on the staff of Mikhail Borodin, the Comintern agent to the Guomindang. He gathered around him a group of young Vietnamese and formed the Association of Revolutionary Vietnamese Youth, the forerunner of the ICP. In 1927 Chiang Kai Shek, leader of the Guomindang and soon to be President of China, turned on the Communists and chased Borodin and his group out of China. Ho spent two years wandering around, but without his direction the Communist movement split into three factions. In May 1929, Ho called these factions together in a meeting at a football stadium in Hong Kong and formed the Indo-Chinese Communist Party.

DOCUMENT STUDY

Founding of the Communist Party of Indo China (February 1930)

“Workers, peasants, soldiers, youth, and pupils!
Oppressed and exploited compatriots!
Sisters and brothers! Comrades!
Imperialist contradictions were the cause of the 1914–18 World War. After this horrible slaughter, the world was divided into two camps: one is the revolutionary camp including the oppressed colonies and the exploited working class throughout the world. The vanguard force of this camp is the Soviet Union. The other is the counter-revolutionary camp of international capitalism and imperialism whose general staff is the League of Nations.

During this World War, various nations suffered untold losses in property and human lives. The French imperialists were the hardest hit. Therefore, in order to restore the capitalist forces in France, the French imperialists have resorted to every underhand scheme to intensify their capitalist exploitation in Indochina. They set up new factories to exploit the workers with low wages. They plundered the peasants' land to establish plantations and drive them to utter poverty. They levied many heavy taxes. They imposed public loans upon our people. In short, they reduced us to wretchedness.
Workers, peasants, soldiers, youth, pupils!
Oppressed and exploited compatriots!

The Communist Party of Indochina is founded. It is the party of the working class. It will help the proletarian class lead the revolution in order to struggle for all the oppressed and exploited people. From now on we must join the Party, help it and follow it in order to implement the following slogans:

1 To overthrow French imperialism, feudalism, and the reactionary Vietnamese capitalist class.
2 To make Indochina completely independent.
3 To establish a worker-peasant and soldier government.
4 To confiscate the banks and other enterprises belonging to the imperialists and put them under the control of the worker-peasant and soldier government.
5 To confiscate all of the plantations and property belonging to the imperialists and the Vietnamese reactionary capitalist class and distribute them to poor peasants.
6 To implement the eight hour working day.
7 To abolish public loans and poll tax. To waive unjust taxes hitting the poor people.
8 To bring back all freedom to the masses.
9 To carry out universal education.
10 To implement equality between man and woman. ”

- At which groups in Vietnamese society is Ho Chi Minh aiming this statement? Why would it appeal to them? Which groups is he not concerned about? Why?
- Ho's interpretation of historical events such as World War I and its aftermath is different from most Western interpretations. What evidence is there to support Ho's views?
- Which aspects of his policies are nationalist and which are Communist? Would Ho see nationalism or Communism as the more important?
- In what ways did the ICP and the VNQDD differ? Compare their support, their aims and their methods.

ICP, 1930–1939

In February 1930, the ICP decided that its first action should be in an area where the Communists could expect to be strong, but where the French were weak. It sent organisers into the Nghe Tinh province in Central Vietnam to agitate on local issues such as high salt prices and low workers' pay. In September 1930 they staged their first protest, a march of 6000 peasants to the provincial capital. The French sent aircraft to bomb the march, and about 200 peasants were killed.

Other attempts by the Communists during 1931–1932 were similarly suppressed. Leading Communists, Pham Van Dong and Le Duc Tho, spent four years on the prison island of Poulo Condore. Ho Chi Minh was arrested in Hong Kong and spent some time in prison. British justice prevented him from being extradited to Vietnam as requested by the French. The Communist organisation went underground, in some places functioning as rural friendly societies. Despite all the efforts of the French, the Communist Party survived. With the failure of other Vietnamese political groups, the nationalist movement was clearly under Communist control at the start of World War II.

WORLD WAR II

The situation in Indo China was changed forever when France was invaded by Nazi Germany and surrendered to Germany in May 1940. The Vichy Government was set up and was allowed to rule southern France as long as it supported Germany. France came under the direct control of Germany, which was an ally of Japan. The Japanese wanted Indo China, and the French were hardly in a position to resist.

The French administrators and part of the army stayed on in Indo China during the war and continued to run the country. However, with the fall of France the Japanese made increasing claims on Indo China, firstly moving into the area north of Hanoi. By late 1941, with the compliance of the French, the Japanese had gained free use of Vietnamese ports, railways, roads and airfields to help in their expansion through the rest of South East Asia. This arrangement suited the Japanese, who were able to get what they wanted without having to use their own troops.

This situation lasted until early 1945 when it became clear that the Japanese would lose. The French started a token resistance to the Japanese, perhaps to ease their conscience for their collaboration. The Japanese acted quickly, and on 9 March rounded up all the French, disarmed them and put them in prison. Having wiped out French power, they ruled directly until the end of the war, with Bao Dai confirmed as their emperor.

During the war the Japanese had forced many peasants to replace their rice crop with commodities that the Japanese wanted, principally jute and peanuts. In early 1945, they started to take whatever rice they could find to store it for their troops. Floods added to the problems caused by these Japanese policies and by mid-1945 famine was widespread through northern Vietnam. Two million out of a population of 10 million died as a result.

The Viet Minh

Ho slipped quietly back into Vietnam in 1940, for the first time since 1912, to set up a 'soviet' in the mountainous area just south of the Chinese border. In May 1941, he called a meeting to form the League for Vietnamese Independence, the Viet Minh. This was a broad organisation set up to fight both the Japanese and the French. The emphasis was deliberately placed on nationalism, not Communism.

During World War II, the US Office of Strategic Services (OSS) trained Ho Chi Minh's forces in the jungles of North Vietnam. The OSS later became the CIA (Patti Collection)

DOCUMENT STUDY

Founding of the Vietnam Doc-Lap Dong Minh Hoi (June 1941)*

"Elders! Prominent personalities! Intellectuals, peasants, workers, traders, and soldiers! Dear compatriots!

Since the French were defeated by the Germans, their forces have been completely disintegrated. However, with regard to our people, they continue to plunder us pitilessly, suck all our blood, and carry out a barbarous policy of all-out terrorism and massacre. Concerning their foreign policy... they heartlessly offer our interests to Japan. As a result, our people suffer under a double yoke: they serve not only as buffaloes and horses to the French invaders but also as slaves to the Japanese plunderers...

Rich people, soldiers, workers, peasants, intellectuals, employees, traders, youth, and women who warmly love your country! At the present time national liberation is the most important problem. Let us unite together! As one in mind and strength we shall overthrow the Japanese and French and their jackals in order to save people from the situation between boiling water and burning heat.

* Revolutionary League for the Independence of Vietnam (Viet Minh)

Dear compatriots!

National salvation is the common cause to the whole of our people. Every Vietnamese must take part in it. He who has money will contribute his money, he who has strength will contribute his strength, he who has talent will contribute his talent. I pledge to use all my modest abilities to follow you, and am ready for the last sacrifice.

Revolutionary fighters!

The hour has struck! Raise aloft the insurrectionary banner and guide the people throughout the country to overthrow the Japanese and French! The sacred call of the fatherland is resounding in your ears; the blood of our heroic predecessors who sacrificed their lives is stirring in your hearts! The fighting spirit of the people is displayed everywhere before you! Let us rise up quickly! Compatriots throughout the country, rise up quickly! Unite with each other, unify your action to overthrow the Japanese and the French. Victory to Vietnam's Revolution!

Victory to the World's Revolution! ”

The selection is from a letter dated 6 June 1941, of Nguyen Ai Quoc (Ho Chi Minh), in Ho Chi Minh, *Selected Works*, 4 vols., Hanoi, 1960–2), II, 151–4

- At which groups is Ho aiming this statement? Why is he now appealing to different groups than he did in 1930?
- Compare the type of language he uses in this statement and the one on pages 17–18.
- Is Ho more concerned with nationalism or Communism? Why?

Ho then left Vietnam to seek help for the Viet Minh from the Chinese Nationalists. They still thought that the VNQDD should be the main anti-Japanese force in Vietnam, and imprisoned Ho for thirteen months. When they realised that the Viet Minh was the only group with any influence, they released Ho and reached an uneasy agreement to work together against the Japanese.

While Ho was in China, his offsider, Vo Nguyen Giap, took his ideas and put them into practice. Giap helped to develop the Viet Minh and spread its influence. He trained military groups and propaganda bands and sent them further and further into Vietnam. He understood how to exploit the Viet Minh's political superiority against the French military superiority.

By early 1945, the Viet Minh had 5000 members strategically placed across the country and was in an excellent position to extend its power when the French collapsed in March 1945. The Americans now needed Ho and his Viet Minh, and airdropped 5000 weapons to them. By June 1945, they had taken over six northern provinces from the Japanese, and were the only native Vietnamese military force.

Review

- How did the actions of the French and the Japanese help to develop nationalism in Vietnam?
- How did the Communists gain control of the nationalist movement?
- What were the VNQDD, the ICP and the Viet Minh?

DECLARATION OF INDEPENDENCE

Japan's defeat was greatly hastened by the dropping of atomic bombs on Hiroshima on 6 August 1945 and Nagasaki three days later. Ho seized this opportunity to fill the power vacuum that would be created by Japan's defeat, and to take power before the French could return. This policy, as outlined by Ho at a meeting of the ICP on 13 August, was:

> "to lead the masses in insurrection in order to disarm the Japanese before the arrival of the Allied forces in Indo-China; to wrest power from the Japanese and their puppet stooges and finally, as the people's power, to welcome the Allied forces coming to disarm the Japanese troops stationed in Indo-China."

Quoted from B. Fall in Asprey, *War in the Shadows*, p. 625

Six days later the Viet Minh moved into Hanoi, and on 26 August into Saigon. Emperor Bao Dai sent a message to the French advising them not to return. He then asked the Viet Minh to form a government, before he abdicated

This painting, now in a Hanoi museum, shows Ho Chi Minh announcing the Declaration of Independence in Hanoi, 2 September 1945

as emperor. In Confucian terms, the Mandate of Heaven was being passed from Bao Dai to Ho Chi Minh. On 2 September in Hanoi, Ho proclaimed the formation of the Democratic Republic of Vietnam, with himself as President, and issued a Declaration of Independence.

DOCUMENT STUDY

Declaration of Independence of the Democratic Republic of Vietnam (2 September 1945)

> 'All men are created equal. They are endowed by their Creator with certain inalienable rights, among these are Life, Liberty, and the pursuit of Happiness.'
>
> This immortal statement was made in the Declaration of Independence of the United States of America in 1776. In a broader sense, this means: All the peoples on the earth are equal from birth, all the peoples have a right to live, to be happy and free.
>
> The Declaration of the French Revolution made in 1791 on the Rights of Man and the Citizen also states: 'All men are born free and with equal rights, and must always remain free and have equal rights.'
>
> Those are undeniable truths...
>
> From the autumn of 1940, our country had in fact ceased to be a French colony and had become a Japanese possession.
>
> After the Japanese had surrendered to the Allies, our whole people rose to regain our national sovereignty and to found the Democratic Republic of Vietnam.
>
> The truth is that we have wrested our independence from the Japanese and not from the French.
>
> The French have fled, the Japanese have capitulated, Emperor Bao Dai has abdicated. Our people have broken the chains which for nearly a century have fettered them and have won independence for the Fatherland. Our people at the same time have overthrown the monarchic regime that has reigned supreme for dozens of centuries. In its place has been established the present Democratic Republic...
>
> We are convinced that the Allied nations which at Tehran and San Francisco have acknowledged the principles of self-determination and equality of nations, will not refuse to acknowledge the independence of Vietnam.
>
> A people who have courageously opposed French domination for more than eight years, a people who have fought side by side with the Allies against the Fascists during these last years, such a people must be free and independent.

Ho Chi Minh, *Selected Works*, 4 vols., Hanoi, 1960–2, III, pp. 17–21

- Why does Ho Chi Minh quote from the American and the French Declarations?
- Whom is he trying to impress with his Declaration?
- How convincing are the arguments that he uses for Vietnamese independence?
- Does Ho make any reference to Communist aims? Why?

THE FRENCH RETURN

The Allied powers had agreed at Potsdam in July 1945 that they would help each other to reclaim their colonial possessions, and they were certainly not going to let Vietnam slip away. British troops were to move into the South and the Chinese Nationalists into the North, to disarm the Japanese and keep control until the French could return.

The British arrived in the South without enough troops to control the chaotic situation. They released French soldiers from prison, who then added to the chaos by going on a rampage. The Viet Minh, who were not as organised or as popular in the South, added to their unpopularity by encouraging the Binh Xuyen gang to kill 150 French and Eurasian civilians. The British commander then allowed the French troops to eject the Viet Minh from the South. This held the situation until the first French troops arrived in early October to re-establish their power, at least in Saigon if not in the villages.

In the North, a disorganised rabble of 200 000 Nationalist Chinese soldiers arrived, supposedly to hold it until the French returned. As historian, Stanley Karnow, described them, 'They resembled a horde of human locusts. Hungry, tattered and even barefoot... they had plundered villages during their march down from China... Once in Hanoi, they continued to pillage promiscuously.'[1]

The Chinese commander had no great interest in the return of the French, and tried to do a deal with Ho. Ho was more cautious, telling a friend that, 'It is better to sniff the French dung for a while than to eat China's all our lives'.[2] As Ho did not have enough power to throw out the Chinese, he started to negotiate with the French. An agreement was reached in March 1946 whereby France recognised Vietnam as an independent state within the French Union, and Ho would allow 25 000 French troops into Vietnam for five years.

Support for Ho Chi Minh varied amongst the major powers:

Soviet Union: The USSR would not support Ho Chi Minh. They had agreed to France returning, and were burdened with their own problems after the war.

China: After the war, civil war developed between Mao Zedong's Communists and the Nationalists (Guomindang). Ho had no contact with Mao, and the Nationalists were strongly against the Communists.

Britain: They wanted the European powers to reclaim their empires. They supported the French, and even rearmed some Japanese to help remove the Viet Minh.

United States: American advisers in Vietnam recommended that the US support Ho Chi Minh, but President Truman was new to the job and had no real policy. Truman needed French support in Europe.

Ho Chi Minh appears to have been favourably inclined towards the United States. It is possible he had lived in New York for a while, and he showed a lively interest in America. His Declaration of Independence borrowed heavily from the United States' example. In August 1945, he stated that he would welcome a million US soldiers and that he saw the United States as a friend.

The Office of Strategic Services (OSS) was the forerunner of the CIA. Major Archimedes Patti of the OSS met with Ho Chi Minh in April 1945 and they reached an informal agreement about helping each other to defeat the Japanese. When Ho declared independence in September, OSS agents reported that the Vietnamese were determined to maintain their independence even at the cost of their lives. President Truman had suddenly assumed office on the death of Roosevelt in April and Vietnam was not at the top of his list of priorities. He had also agreed at Potsdam that France should return. Disagreements within the State Department meant that the USA had no clear policy on Vietnam. So, despite some sympathy for Ho Chi Minh, the US lost the opportunity of making him an ally. As the Cold War developed so did US distrust of Ho.

> "I have always shared the belief of many, if not most, observers who were in Indochina at the time that a serious mistake was made by both the French and the Americans, especially by the dominant French policymakers in Paris, in not dealing more realistically with Ho in 1945 and 1946, when there was a strong possibility that... the whole course of events might thereby have been altered and a great deal of bloodshed averted..."

Robert Shaplen, *The Lost Revolution: Vietnam 1945–65*, Andre Deutsch, London, 1966 p. 30

Discuss

- What type of 'deal' could the French and Americans have made with Ho? What type of state might have been created?
- Would Ho have been genuine in seeking US support? Why didn't he gain it?

Review

- What arrangements were made by the Allies to allow the French to return to Vietnam?
- How did the French regain control in the South, and later on, in the North?

Discuss

- Ho left Vietnam in 1911 and apart from a brief time in 1941, did not return until 1945. Why, then, did he emerge as the undisputed leader of the Vietnamese in 1945?
- Why was Ho Chi Minh a Communist? How would Communism help to solve Vietnam's problems?

FAILURE OF NEGOTIATIONS

The agreement of March 1946 was seen by both the Viet Minh and the French as temporary. Ho had to assure his disappointed supporters that he had not sold them out. France's attitude to Vietnam hardened during 1946, as French pride started to re-emerge after the years of occupation by the Germans. Regaining control of Vietnam would help to restore the national pride that had been so badly battered. The French also felt that it was their duty to bring the benefits of French civilisation to the 'inferior' Vietnamese.

Ho Chi Minh addresses an audience in Paris in 1946. His attempts to negotiate with the French failed and he left in September (AP/Wide World Photos)

HO CHI MINH (1890–1969)

Ho was born Nguyen Tat Thanh in 1890. His father was a relatively wealthy peasant who was very strongly nationalist, and who was dismissed from his position as mandarin because he refused to learn French. Ho grew up at a time when resentment at French rule was developing, and in a family environment that encouraged such resentment. He left Vietnam in 1911 on a French boat, working as a kitchen hand, and spent some time in London before settling in Paris during World War I. He joined the French Socialist Party, and was a founding member of the Communist Party when it split with the Socialists.

At the Versailles Peace Conference in 1919, Ho was a one-man delegation pushing the case for Vietnamese independence. He did not gain a hearing at Versailles, but he did establish a reputation amongst the many Vietnamese in Paris. This reputation spread to Vietnam as these people returned and as his writings became widely known. In 1924, Ho moved to Moscow to further his Communist studies, and the next year he was sent to China as a Comintern agent. Ho's principal motive throughout remained the same as that of his father: independence and unity. His experiences in Europe had added Communism as another aim, although he probably looked on Communism as a means of achieving his primary aim of nationalism. He realised that only Communism could be sufficiently disciplined and brutal to remove the French and restructure the country.

Ho maintained an air of mystery about his movements and his private life. The French, and later the Americans, underestimated the appeal that he had to his people.

> “He was the gentle Vietnamese, humble, soft-spoken, mocking his own position, always seen in the simplest garb, his dress made him barely distinguishable from the poorest peasant — a style that Westerners for many years mocked, laughing at the lack of trappings of power, of uniform, of style, until one day they woke up and realised that this very simplicity, this cult of simplicity, this capacity to walk simply among his own people was basic to his success.”

Halberstam, *Ho*, p. 13

Ho went to France in May 1946 to carry on the negotiations with the French. The longer he stayed, the more it became obvious that the French were not serious. As David Halberstam puts it: 'To the French, a war was unthinkable, but the alternative, giving away independence to little yellow men who could easily be dominated, was even more unthinkable'.[3]

Negotiations dragged on until September when Ho left Paris, not wanting war, but expecting it. In his absence, General Giap had been rapidly developing the Viet Minh so that it now had 100000 under arms. Scattered outbreaks of violence occurred between them and the French. On 23 November, the French bombarded Haiphong and cleared the Viet Minh from the city. The Viet Minh decided that the time had come to act, and in December attacked Hanoi. Giap issued a virtual declaration of war. Hanoi became a battleground, but the Viet Minh was finally driven from the city. The French Indo China War was under way.

Structured questions

- How had World War II affected the Indo-Chinese Communist Party?
- (a) Why did Ho Chi Minh declare the independence of Vietnam in September 1945?
  (b) How much support was there for this Declaration from within Vietnam and from other countries?
- How did this Declaration of Independence lead to the outbreak of fighting by the end of 1946?

KEY EVENTS

1927 VNQDD formed.
1929 ICP formed.
1930 *February*: VNQDD uprising crushed.
1941 *May*: France defeated by Germany.
September: Ho declares Vietnamese independence.
October: French return to South Vietnam.
1945 *March*: Japanese take full control of Vietnam from the French.
August: Japan defeated.
1946 *March*: Agreement allows French troops to return to North Vietnam.
November: French attack on Haiphong.
December: Viet Minh attack on Hanoi. Start of the French Indo China War.

THE FRENCH WAR

CHAPTER FOUR

1947–1954

FROM THE START, the French made the basic mistake of looking for military solutions to political problems. They also underestimated the strength of the Viet Minh and the support it would gain from the ordinary Vietnamese. These mistakes were later repeated by the Americans. Neither the French nor the Americans succeeded in setting up a government that was a credible alternative to Communism. The ordinary Vietnamese had no real interest in Communism, but simply wanted *Doc Lap* (independence). Involvement by the French and the Americans emphasised that they could only achieve Doc Lap if they supported the Viet Minh, and later the Viet Cong.

Ho Chi Minh realised that Communist theory had little appeal. His rallying call to the people when the fighting began in December 1946 avoids any mention of Communism:

> "... Compatriots! Rise up!
> Men and women, old and young, regardless of creeds, political parties, or nationalities, all the Vietnamese must stand up to fight the French colonialists to save the Fatherland. Those who have rifles will use their rifles; those who have swords will use their swords; those who have no swords will use spades, hoes, or sticks. Everyone must endeavor to oppose the colonialists and save his country."

Ho Chi Minh, *Selected Works*, III, pp. 81–2

Ho also realised that to succeed he needed the support of the peasants, and their major concern was getting enough land to farm.* Forty per cent of Vietnam's riceland was owned by 0.25 per cent of the population. Ho promised the peasants land reform and in areas under Viet Minh control land redistribution was carried out. Up to 1949, there was not as much emphasis on

* Control of the villages was vital to the control of the Vietnamese people. Neither the French nor later the Americans were able to achieve this control. The French did not have enough Vietnamese-speaking officials to meet the villagers on their own level. The American soldiers were only there for twelve months and were not interested in village life during that time. Both the Viet Minh and the Viet Cong were able to use their local contacts, helped by selective assassinations of pro-French or corrupt village officials, to gain the support (or at least the neutrality) of the great majority of villages.

land reform policy, because Ho was trying to gain support from all sections of Vietnamese society. This changed in 1949 with the victory of the Communists in China. The Viet Minh became more openly a Communist group, and Ho abandoned his efforts to win support from Vietnam's small middle class. Much greater emphasis was placed on land reform. These promises, according to Gabriel Kolko, were important elements in the Communist success at Dien Bien Phu in 1954.

> "The mass mobilization of the peasantry saw the Party through Dien Bien Phu and its remarkable triumph over France after one decade. The thousands of peasants who died there were patriots, but they were also often first and foremost fighting for a revolution in land relations. That incentive would later succeed again and again, and it would also evoke spontaneous, dynamic mass action and devotion to the cause. The peasant would fight for land, with or without the Party, and that passion could overshadow ideology and discipline."

Gabriel Kolko, *Vietnam, Anatomy of War 1940–1975*, Unwin, London, 1987, p. 61

THE VIET MINH

The Viet Minh developed into such a powerful force largely because it concentrated on both political and military aspects, whereas the French aimed at military victory and paid little attention to political development. Political training for the Viet Minh soldier was seen as being of more importance than his military training. Political cadres or organisers were attached to all sections of the Viet Minh army. Cadres were also sent to the villages of Vietnam to spread anti-French propaganda and to encourage ideas on land reform.

The revolutionary army also grew from the villages, developing in three separate steps.

> "Irregular village guerrilla units first rooted the army in its social base and provided the institutional foundations for mass mobilisation at higher levels. When enough guerrilla units had been mobilised in a region, people and resources were then channelled into the formation of quasi-regular regional units of up to regimental strength. Finally, mainforce divisions were formed in their turn at the national level."

Greg Lockhart, 'The nature of the Vietnam War', unpublished paper presented to the Macquarie University Conference, 1987

In 1948, Ho Chi Minh set out rules for soldiers that show clearly the type of army that was being developed:

> "*Six forbiddances to the bureaucrats and soldiers*
>
> **1** Not to do what is likely to damage the land and crops or spoil the houses and belongings of the people.
> **2** Not to insist on buying or borrowing what the people are not willing to sell or lend.
> **3** Not to bring living hens into the mountain people's houses.
> **4** Never to break your word.
> **5** Not to give offense to people's faith and customs (such as to lie down

before the altar, to raise the feet over the hearth, to play music in the house, etc.).

6 Not to do or speak what is likely to make people believe that we hold them in contempt.

Six permissibles

1 To help the people in their daily work (harvesting, fetching firewood, carrying water, sewing, etc.).

2 Whenever possible, to buy commodities for those who live far from markets (knives, salt, needles, thread, pen, paper, etc.).

3 In spare time, to tell amusing, simple, and short stories useful to the Resistance, but not betraying secrets.

4 To teach the population the national script and elementary hygiene.

5 To study the customs of each region so as to be acquainted with them in order to create an atmosphere of sympathy first, then gradually to explain to the people to abate their superstitions.

6 To show to the people that you are correct, diligent, and disciplined. ”

Ho Chi Minh, *Selected Works*, pp. 146–7

Many of these rules are similar to Mao Zedong's instructions to the Chinese Red Army.

A Viet Minh leader, Truong-Chinh, explained how important it was to work with the peasants:

“ The people are the eyes and ears of the army, they feed and keep our soldiers. It is they who help the army in sabotage and in battle. The people are the water and our army the fish. The people constitute an inexhaustible source of strength for the army. ”

Truong-Chinh, *Selected Writings*, p. 111–12, as quoted in Kolko, *Vietnam*, p. 43

David Halberstam sums up the appeal of the Viet Minh for the peasants:

“ For a Vietnamese of that generation there was only one question: Which side are you on, the Vietnamese side or the colonialist side? And from this passion, the Vietminh over a period of eight years welded an extraordinary political and military force. To the peasant, consigned by birth to a life of misery, poverty, ignorance, the Vietminh showed a way out. A man could be as good as his innate talent permitted; lack of privilege was for the first time in centuries not a handicap — if anything, it was an asset. One could fight and die serving the nation, liberating both the nation and oneself. Nepotism and privilege, which had dominated the feudal society of the past, were wiped away. One rose only by ability. ”

Halberstam, *Ho*, p. 93

Review

Make a list of the main reasons why the Viet Minh became such 'an extraordinary political and military force' in the period to 1954. Look closely at the reasons why the Vietnamese peasants would support them.

PROGRESS OF THE WAR

General Giap planned that the war would develop in three stages, and it did proceed as he had planned. From the start Giap was setting the pace.

Stage 1: 1947

Retreat and rebuilding for the Viet Minh. The French moved into many areas and tried to re-establish their control. The Viet Minh built up their bases in the secure, mountainous Viet Bac area near the Chinese border.

Stage 2: 1948-1949

The Viet Minh went on the offensive, concentrating on guerrilla attacks with the aim of wearing down the French.

Stage 3: 1950-1951 and 1954

Giap realised that guerrilla attacks would not be sufficient to drive out the French, and that a direct counter-offensive against specific French positions would be needed. He felt confident enough to go on the offensive in 1950, and in October attacked a French force at Cao Bang, near the Chinese border.

> "When the smoke cleared, the French had suffered their greatest colonial defeat since Montcalm had died at Quebec. They had lost 6,000 troops, 13 artillery pieces and 125 mortars, 450 trucks and three armored platoons, 940 machine guns, 1200 sub-machine-guns and more than 8,000 rifles. Their abandoned stocks alone sufficed for the equipment of a whole additional Viet-Minh division."

Bernard Fall, *Street Without Joy*, Schocken, New York, 1972, p. 33

This and other attacks gave the Viet Minh control of the northern part of North Vietnam by early 1951. The French held onto the Red River delta and to South Vietnam, where Viet Minh activities were confined to guerrilla attacks.

The Viet Minh suffered severe setbacks in 1951, and direct attacks on the French were limited during 1952 and 1953. The Viet Minh realised, however, that time was on its side, and that opposition to the war would develop in France the longer it dragged on. Ho Chi Minh had outlined this approach in an interview in 1946 when he compared the French to an elephant and the Vietnamese to a tiger: 'When the elephant is strong and rested near his base we will retreat. And if the tiger ever pauses, the elephant will impale him on his mighty tusks. But the tiger will not pause and the elephant will die of exhaustion and loss of blood.'

Problems for the French

In trying to re-establish their empire, the French were aiming to restore their national pride that had been so badly damaged when they had been defeated and occupied by the Germans in 1941. However, World War II had left France economically weakened and politically unstable and in no fit state to take on a long war. There were frequent changes of government in France. The Communist Party in France regularly gained 25 per cent of the vote, making stable coalition government much more difficult.

The war became known in France as 'the dirty war', and the longer it dragged on, the stronger the opposition became.

The French writer Bernard Fall claimed that 'French opposition to the Indo-China War was widespread and by no means limited to left wing elements'.[1] A future Premier of France, Pierre Mendès-France, opposed the war from 1950. In a speech to Parliament, he said that France should either triple the size of its forces in Vietnam or start negotiations with the Viet Minh.

THE COLD WAR

International developments in 1949–1950 involved Vietnam in the rapidly worsening Cold War, and were a turning point in the fortunes of the Viet Minh. The attitude of the major powers towards Vietnam changed after the Communist victory in China in October 1949 and the start of the Korean War in 1950.

The United States saw these events as further evidence of the worldwide spread of Communism. Anti-Communist hysteria was common in the US and would be whipped up even further during the 1950s by Senator McCarthy. The US had shown no concern for Ho Chi Minh up to 1949, but this now changed rapidly and Ho became identified as part of the Communist conspiracy, cunningly manipulated by Moscow. The domino theory emerged and Indo China became a vital player in the Cold War.

> "The fall of Indochina would undoubtedly lead to the fall of the other mainland states of Southeast Asia,' the Joint Chiefs of Staff argued in April 1950, and with Russia would control 'Asia's war potential... affecting the balance of power.' Not only 'major sources of certain strategic materials' would be lost, but also communication routes."

Kolko, *Vietnam*, p. 75

The United States officially declared that it would stop Communist expansion in South East Asia. From 1950 to 1954 its policy was to avoid direct military intervention but to give every possible support to the French. By 1954, the US was paying for 80 per cent of French expenditure on the war. No US troops were involved but supporting the French was costing US taxpayers $3 million a day.

Mao Zedong recognised the Viet Minh when he came to power and started to give them considerable help. Over the next three years China provided 50 000 tonnes of supplies. According to Robert Shaplen, 'the Viet Minh moved clearly into the world Communist camp, and the Republic in the North was completely taken over by hard-line Communist officials'.[2]

The USSR, on the other hand, recognised the Ho Chi Minh regime in 1950 but played no direct role in Vietnam.

Review

- Outline the three stages of the war.
- How did the war in Vietnam become part of the Cold War?

No alternative government?

The French failed to create in Vietnam a government that the ordinary Vietnamese could consider as an alternative to the Viet Minh. By 1949, they had managed to persuade Bao Dai to resume his role as France's puppet head of state. The French claimed to have handed over independence to Bao Dai, but the Vietnamese did not see it this way and had no confidence in him. After all, he had passed the Mandate of Heaven to Ho Chi Minh in 1945. Bernard Fall wrote in early 1954:

> "A young graduate of the Ecole Militaire Inter-Armes at Dalat said to me: 'How do you think it feels getting oneself killed in the jungle for that man who comes up here to swear us in wearing a Riviera suit, a polka-dot tie, and inch-thick crepe soles?' He was referring to His Majesty Bao-Dai, commander in chief of the Vietnamese forces, who has not yet been seen in the uniform of his army."

Fall, *Vietnam Witness*, p. 15

No serious effort was made to set up a democratic government. Even at the village level, no elections were held until 1953, and even then they only involved 12 per cent of the villages in the North.

DIEN BIEN PHU

In early 1954, the French decided to try and end the war quickly by luring the Viet Minh into a conventional battle. They chose Dien Bien Phu as a place that they would be forced to capture at any cost, at it was within Viet Minh controlled territory and close to the Laotian border. The Viet Minh had extended their activities into Laos during 1953, so the French established a strongly fortified position at Dien Bien Phu to stop this development. However, the French made some serious mistakes in planning for the battle:

- They underestimated the Viet Minh's size and power. They assumed that the Viet Minh would have no heavy artillery or, if they did have any, would not know how to use it.
- Dien Bien Phu was on the floor of a valley, ringed by mountains rising 500 metres over the forts.

Indo China 1953–1954

- It was too far from Hanoi to be given effective air cover. Fighter aircraft could only spend ten minutes over Dien Bien Phu before having to return to Hanoi. The French garrison could only be supplied by air, and they needed 200 tonnes of supplies each day. (Amongst the garrison's supplies were 49 000 bottles of wine.)

General Giap took advantage of most of these blunders by the French. Up to 20 000 peasants were mobilised to carry supplies from China along what later became known as the Ho Chi Minh Trail. A member of the Viet Minh later described the experience:

> "We had to cross mountains and jungles, marching at night and sleeping by day to avoid enemy bombing. We sometimes slept in foxholes, or just by the trail. We each carried a rifle, ammunition, and hand grenades, and our packs contained a blanket, a mosquito net, and a change of clothes. We each had a week's supply of rice, which we refilled at depots along the way. We ate greens and bamboo shoots that we picked in the jungle, and occasionally villagers would give us a bit of meat. I'd been in the Vietminh for nine years by then, and I was accustomed to it."

Karnow, *Vietnam*, p. 191

Several hundred large guns were dug into the mountains, camouflaged from air attack. On 13 March 1954, when the first fogs of the year rolled in, the Viet Minh opened fire. The French artillery commander committed suicide that night. Over the next few weeks the Viet Minh tightened the noose around Dien Bien Phu. Under artillery cover their troops dug trenches ever closer to the French. (The US Government just resisted the temptation to send bombers to help the French.) On 7 May 1954 the French garrison surrendered. The next day the Geneva Conference met for the first time, with the French anxious to get out of Vietnam as soon as possible.

THE GENEVA CONFERENCE

With the Cold War thawing a little after the death of Stalin in 1953, the foreign ministers of the United States, the Soviet Union, Britain and France

A Viet Minh supply train of bicycles and porters crossing a pontoon bridge en route to Dien Bien Phu (Paris-Match)

Ho Chi Minh and his high command planning the battle of Dien Bien Phu in their jungle headquarters. General Giap, the commander of the Viet Minh forces, is on the right (Black Star)

agreed to meet to discuss a possible settlement in Korea and Indo China. The conference met at Geneva from April to July 1954, with nine delegations present. The main decisions were made in secret meetings between the French Premier, Pierre Mendès-France, and the Chinese Foreign Minister, Zhou Enlai. The Chinese were keen to weaken Vietnam by having it divided, and eventually persuaded the French to agree to a plan of partition. The United States and the South Vietnamese delegations refused to sign the final agreements. The Viet Minh were also unhappy, claiming that the Chinese had double-crossed them.

The main outcomes of the Geneva Conference were:

- Vietnam was divided at the Seventeenth Parallel.
- North Vietnam became a Communist state, the Democratic Republic of Vietnam, with Ho Chi Minh as President.
- South Vietnam became an American-supported, anti-Communist state. Ngo Dinh Diem became Prime Minister in 1954 and President in 1956 when Bao Dai was finally pushed out.
- Elections were to be held in 1956 to reunify Vietnam.
- Civilians and soldiers had nine months to move freely between the two areas. Some 850 000 left the North for the South, and only 80 000 went North.

Problems with the settlement

The settlement was more of a ceasefire than a permanent solution. The Viet Minh had fought for unity, and felt resentful that they had been robbed of it at the negotiating table. Ngo Dinh Diem would refuse to take part in the elections in 1956, because it was clear that Ho Chi Minh would have won. The Americans were still obsessed with containing monolithic Communist expansion, and wanted to set up a strong buffer state in the South. They did not want a unified Vietnam, and opposed the 1956 elections.

Review

- List the reasons why the French were defeated. Arrange them in order of importance.
- Why did the United States become involved in Vietnam?
- How did support from Communist China help the Viet Minh in the war?
- List the advantages that the Viet Minh had in the war, and the disadvantages that the French had.
- What were the main decisions made by the Geneva Conference? How likely was it that these decisions would provide a permanent solution?

Discuss

In what ways was the war from 1947 to 1954 a colonial war, a civil war or a revolutionary war?

Research

- Read detailed accounts of the Battle of Dien Bien Phu. As a French soldier trapped there, give your thoughts on the Viet Minh and on your commanders.
- Read Graham Greene's novel, *The Quiet American*.

Structured questions

Read carefully the Six Forbiddances and the Six Permissibles of the Viet Minh (pages 42–43).

- Why would the peasants be likely to support an army that followed these rules?
- What other reasons are there to explain the support that the Viet Minh received from the villagers in Vietnam?
- Why didn't the French receive this support? Does this failure to win support at the village level help to explain the defeat of the French in the war?

THE TWO GENERALS

General Vo Nguyen Giap was undoubtedly responsible for the defeat of the French at Dien Bien Phu. He was also the chief military strategist in the war against the Americans up to 1975, and played a large part in their defeat. Stanley Karnow refers to him as one of the century's most spectacular soldiers.

Giap was born in 1912 in Central Vietnam, one of the country's harshest provinces. He first became involved in anti-French protests at the age of 14. His father managed to scrape together enough money to have him educated in Law at Hanoi University. After graduating, he continued his anti-French activities and scraped a living together by working as a history teacher.

His attitude hardened in 1941 when his wife and infant son died in a French prison, and his wife's sister was guillotined in Saigon. Giap then joined Ho in China where he helped to form the Viet Minh. Ho sent him back to Vietnam to build up the military organisation of the Viet Minh.

Giap's opponent at Dien Bien Phu was the complete opposite. Colonel Christian Marie Ferdinand de la Croix de Castries could trace his military ancestry back 800 years. 'Irresistible to women and ridden with gambling debts, he had been a champion horseman, dare-devil pilot, and courageous commando, his body scarred by three wounds.'[3] He declined the offer of more battalions before the battle started.

General Vo Nguyen Giap (US Defense Department)

Far right. *Colonel Christian de Castries, French commander at Dien Bien Phu, was a romantic cavalry officer who had been wounded and decorated in World War II (Popperfoto)*

'THE ONLY BOY WE GOT'

CHAPTER FIVE

1954–1963

THE UNITED STATES maintained its strong influence in South Vietnam after the withdrawal of the French. The Americans saw Vietnam as an important element in their policy of containing Communism. President Eisenhower made this clear in 1954 when he said that if Vietnam fell to Communism, then the other Asian states would fall, like dominoes stood on their ends, until even Australia was under threat. The United States would be forced back to Hawaii, as it was before World War II.

The United States thought that this domino effect would take place through external invasion, not from internal guerrilla warfare. It expected that at some stage the North Vietnamese Army, backed by the Chinese, would invade the South across the Seventeenth Parallel. Because of this, it helped the South Vietnamese Army to develop so that it could deal with a conventional war, not guerrilla attacks.

United States policy under both Presidents Eisenhower and Kennedy was based on the assumption that the US had to stick with Ngo Dinh Diem no matter what:

> “... during a visit to Saigon in 1961, Lyndon Johnson, then vice-president, had compared Diem to Churchill. 'Did you really mean it?' I asked Johnson aboard his airplane later. 'Shit,' he drawled. 'Diem's the only boy we got out there.'”

Karnow, *Vietnam*, p. 214

This attitude gave Diem free rein. By 1961 he had set up a clearly totalitarian regime, but the US stuck with him as their basic interests coincided. The United States obviously thought it more important for Diem to stop Communism than for him to make any attempt to set up a democratic government in South Vietnam. In 1955, the US sent $100 million in aid and, over the next three years, paid two-thirds of South Vietnam's budget. Many US civilian advisers were sent out to help reconstruct the country. Diem accepted the US dollars, but generally rejected the advice.

Review

What were the three basic assumptions of United States policy? Were these assumptions correct?

Discuss

- Compare US support for Diem's regime with that given to Ferdinand Marcos in the Philippines. Are there any similarities between the Marcos family and the Diem dynasty?
- What instances have there been of the US backing a leader because of his firm anti-Communism, and disregarding his denial of democracy?

Diem's successes	*Diem's failures*
• Established a totalitarian regime • Kept US support until October 1963	• An effective army was not created • No meaningful land reforms were carried out • Did not introduce any form of representative government • Alienated almost every important group: Buddhists, peasants, Chinese, Army, Montagnards

A TOTALITARIAN REGIME

By the time John Kennedy became US President in January 1961, South Vietnam was clearly a totalitarian state. There were an estimated 150 000 political prisoners, only a minority of whom were Communists. No book or newspaper could be published unless it was first passed by the censors. Public meetings were banned, and even weddings and funerals required twenty-four hours notice. The Bill for the Protection of Morality, introduced in 1962, banned all forms of dancing. With no opposition to Diem allowed, the only way of removing him was by coup, not by the ballot box.

In 1956, Diem abolished elections in the villages for the village officials. Instead, they were to be appointed by the Diem Government. According to Gabriel Kolko, 'These were mostly Catholics and/or Diem cronies from the Hué region, and all were out to make money. As outsiders they and their police personified the RVN's [Republic of Vietnam] daily oppression and corruption over the peasantry.'[1]

Diem was supposed to have carried out land redistribution, but only a quarter of a million hectares was distributed and most of this went to Catholics or ex-soldiers. Any peasants who did get land had to pay for it within six years. Earlier land redistribution by the Viet Minh had been free, but Diem declared all of these land transfers illegal.

Ngo Dinh Diem in his palace in Saigon. Diem kept himself aloof from the people, preferring to mix only with his family and close aides (Howard Sochurek, courtesy Life *magazine)*

NGO DINH DIEM

Diem's main qualifications to be Prime Minister were that he was anti-Communist, anti-French and was well known in Washington. He was not well known in Vietnam, and had not taken part in the war against the French. He came from an aristocratic Catholic family and had first made a name for himself as an administrator for the French. In 1933 he was appointed as a minister in Bao Dai's puppet government, but resigned shortly afterwards when he realised that the French would not give him any real power. In 1946 he tried to establish an anti-Communist organisation, and the next year he set up an anti-French political party. The Viet Minh sentenced him to death *in absentia* in 1950 and, when the French decided not to give him police protection, he left for the United States where he spent two years in a monastery. He also used this time to make contacts with important US politicians, including John F. Kennedy.

Diem returned in 1954 as Prime Minister, but lacked popular support, gaining most of his backing from the Catholic minority. This did not stop him from arranging, with CIA support, a vote of 98.2 per cent for himself in the 1955 elections. Violent resistance to Diem from the Binh Xuyen, Cao Dai and Hoa Hao sects was crushed in 1955, allowing him to consolidate a regime based on power, not popularity.

Diem passionately believed in his country, but his view of Vietnam was old fashioned. He saw it as a Confucian society in which everyone knew their place and there was no twentieth century nonsense about democracy. Although his thinking was Confucian, he was a deeply religious Catholic who lived very much the solitary life of a monk. There is no evidence of any personal corruption, although he allowed corruption to flourish among his family and supporters.

> "He was a short, broadly built man with a round face and a shock of black hair, who walked and moved jerkily, as if on strings. He always dressed in white and looked as if he were made out of ivory. His self-absorption became apparent as soon as he started to speak, identifying himself and his cause with the nation. He indulged in few amenities of greeting, and since he was a compulsive talker, with whom it was impossible to have an interview — one had an audience; in fact, one *was* an audience — a single question was likely to provoke a dissertation of an hour or more."

Shaplen, *The Lost Revolution*, p. 104

Review

- Why was Ngo Dinh Diem not acceptable to most Vietnamese?

Ngo Dinh Diem (left) with his immediate family. Behind him is his brother and chief adviser, Ngo Dinh Nhu. The woman in the centre is Madame Nhu, his powerful sister-in-law. The oldest brother is Archbishop Thuc, at the rear (Michigan State University Archives and Historical Collections)

The Army

From 1956, the United States took over the job of reorganising the Vietnamese Army. The most able officers were sent for training in the United States in conventional warfare. This created an officer class, untrained to handle guerrilla attacks.

As Diem's unpopularity grew, he had to guard against possible overthrow from the Army. As Robert Shaplen says: 'Diem and Nhu [his brother] could no longer afford to select military commanders on the basis of ability, but solely by virtue of their loyalty. This naturally tended to inhibit the efficiency of the Army.'[2] An attempted coup in 1960 by sections of the Army was only narrowly defeated. The ineffectiveness of Diem's army was clearly shown in a battle at Ap Bac in January 1963. Three battalions, with support from US helicopters, surrounded a Viet Cong force one-tenth that size. Nine Viet Cong were killed, and 400 ARVN soldiers killed or wounded. The ARVN troops were led by Catholics promoted for their loyalty to Diem.

Review

- Find a definition of totalitarianism. In what ways does Diem's regime fit your definition?

THE VIET CONG

Resistance to Diem developed among the remnants of the Viet Minh. Some of the 80 000 who had gone North in 1954 started to drift back and, along with the ex-Viet Minh who had remained, provided a focus for resistance to Diem. They became labelled the *Viet Cong* (Vietnamese Communists) although, at least in the early stages, there were still a number of non-Communists in the movement. Viet Cong was not a name they gave themselves. At first, they were very loosely organised. From 1957, they started to return to the agitation-propaganda methods that had been so successful against the French.

Cadres moved gradually into the villages to carry out the propaganda work. They started by gaining the confidence of the villagers and convinced them of how they were being exploited. The peasants were promised real independence for their country, peace and land reform:

> “The peasant now had something to fight for. Now, he would lend his children to the Viet Cong, the younger as messengers, the older as fighters. Now he would donate to the cause, now he would pay taxes, now he would supply food and sanctuary and guides who would help guerrillas transit twenty-five miles of tortuous terrain in five hours of night marches.”

Asprey, *War in the Shadows*, p. 1084

Selective assassinations of village officials were carried out, rising to a level of 4000 a year by 1961. Quite often, this gave the peasants some relief from a repressive government, as well as showing the power of the Viet Cong. Teachers were also a target, often because they were seen as agents of the Diem Government, and this forced the closure of 600 schools. Viet Cong methods were insidious and effective. By 1961 they claimed to control almost the entire countryside at night, and over two-thirds of it during the day.

Support from the North

It is likely that the North Vietnamese Government gave encouragement but no material support to the Viet Cong up to 1959. Ho's priority was to develop the North and consolidate Communist power and reforms there before he tried to unify Vietnam. However, the Viet Cong movement grew more rapidly than Ho had anticipated. In December 1960, Ho announced the formation of the National Liberation Front (NLF) to bring together the different groups opposing Diem. Leadership of the NLF stayed in the South, and it was largely a southern Communist organisation, although it was guided from the North. The Viet Cong received weapons from the North along the Ho Chi Minh Trail from 1959. The formation of the NLF then represented a clear declaration of a war of national independence on the Diem Government and its United States backers.

Review

- Explain the difference between the Viet Minh, the Viet Cong and the National Liberation Front.
- Why did the Communists decide to resume the war against the South?

DIEM REGIME IN DECLINE

Strategic hamlets

Diem and his brother, Nhu, devised the strategic hamlet program in 1961 to try and win back control of the villages. The idea was to put the peasants into fortified villages surrounded by ditches, barbed wire and spiked bamboo. This was supposed to cut them off from the Viet Cong. Instead, the peasants greatly resented being uprooted and forced to move into what seemed to them to be concentration camps rather than sanctuaries. When the Viet Cong attacked the strategic hamlets, the peasants usually opened the gates and let them in.

To isolate peasants from the Viet Cong guerrillas, the South Vietnamese Government built fortified enclosures called 'strategic hamlets'. But this alienated many peasants, who resented being moved from their native villages.

Kennedy's dilemma

When John F. Kennedy took over in January 1961, he had to prove his credentials as a Cold War warrior. Nixon had accused him of being soft on Communism, and Nixon had very nearly won the election. Kennedy agreed to allow an attempted invasion of Cuba by Cuban exiles, based in Florida, to go ahead in March. This Bay of Pigs invasion was a fiasco, and helped to convince the Soviet leader, Nikita Khrushchev, that Kennedy could be pushed around. Khrushchev further humiliated Kennedy at a summit meeting in 1961. United States credibility around the world was in danger, and Kennedy became convinced it could not be damaged any further. Vietnam was to be one place where he could restore this credibility.

Diem was obviously in trouble in early 1961, and Kennedy was under a lot of pressure to increase US support for him, which then stood at 700 military advisers. Very rapidly, this number was built up to 3000, and within two years had reached 16 000 advisers. It became almost impossible for these advisers not to take part in actual fighting. At the Battle of Ap Bac, for example, US pilots flew the Vietnamese soldiers into battle, and five Americans were killed. The increase in troop numbers was kept secret because it was outside decisions made at Geneva. Involvement of US troops in the fighting was also kept secret. So the pattern for future American involvement was set early in the Kennedy years — secrecy and escalation to protect US credibility.

The Buddhist revolt

Diem did not set out to discriminate against the Buddhists, but because the Catholics were so favoured it was inevitable that the Buddhists would suffer. Catholics were given the best government jobs, the top army positions, and the best land. In building the strategic hamlets, the Catholics were often let off doing any of the hard work, while the Buddhists had to take time off from their farming to dig ditches and build their own concentration camps. The last straw came in May 1963 when they were refused permission to display Buddhist flags or have meetings on the anniversary of Buddha's birthday. Government troops fired on a protest march, and nine were killed. This set off a wave of protest throughout Vietnam which the Buddhist leaders exploited for maximum publicity.

On 11 June a 66-year-old Buddhist monk, Thich Quan Duc, soaked himself with petrol on a Saigon street corner and calmly lit a match. A photographer had been tipped off about the event, and his photo caused a great stir around the world. Six more monks committed public suicide in the next few weeks. Diem's sister-in-law, the infamous Madame Nhu, described them as 'barbecues'. Her husband, Ngo Dinh Nhu, made the situation worse in August when he raided Buddhist pagodas across Vietnam, and several hundred Buddhist priests were arrested.

President Kennedy was greatly influenced by the suicides, and his approach to the Vietnam issue started to change. He recalled Ambassador Nolting and

A young Buddhist monk keeps his cross-legged position as flames engulf him. Nearby observers heard no sound from the monk. His self-immolation was one of several in 1963 that influenced the US Government's decision not to continue backing Diem's regime (UPI/ Bettmann Newsphotos)

replaced him with Henry Cabot Lodge. He also started to look for ways in which the US could withdraw from Vietnam. In a speech in September, Kennedy suggested that a change of policy and people was needed in the Saigon Government. This was a clear hint to Diem that he should get rid of his brother, but Diem did not act.

Assassinations

Ambassador Lodge was given wide powers to act, and to cut off US aid to Diem if he thought that it was necessary. Some Vietnamese generals approached Lodge privately and advised him that they might have to take matters into their own hands and stage a coup. Lodge let it be known to the generals that the US would not interfere in any coup, and would continue aid to a new government if Diem was removed. A CIA agent, Lucien Conein, met secretly with a representative of the plotters, who kept him well advised on the planning for the coup.

The coup began during the afternoon of 1 November when troops moved into Saigon. Within an hour, they had occupied the key positions and surrounded the presidential palace. They called on Diem and Nhu to resign, but they refused. At 3.30 the next morning twenty-four tanks attacked the palace, but Diem and Nhu had escaped through a secret exit to a house in the Chinese section of Saigon. They then telephoned the generals to offer to resign, but when troops called for them they had fled. They were found hiding in a Catholic church, and were placed in an armoured personnel carrier. On the way back to the palace, Diem was shot in the head and Nhu was stabbed to death.

Shaplen, *The Lost Revolution*, p. 211

" Although the Americans were not happy about the murder of Diem — they had less qualms about Nhu — the coup was executed with their full knowledge and with their consent. The approval given by Washington to go ahead, in the first place, and the carefully guarded role then played by Ambassador Lodge, acting through the American go-between, were crucial. "

Review

- Read detailed accounts of the coup in books such as *Vietnam: A History* by Stanley Karnow, and *Vietnam: The Ten Thousand Day War* by Michael Maclear. Do their views of the coup agree with that of Robert Shaplen?
- How and why did the United States increase its involvement in Vietnam's affairs?
- How did the Buddhist revolt help to destroy Diem's Government?

Research

- What were the Cao Dai, Hoa Hao and Binh Xuyen?

Structured questions

- Describe the events leading up to the assassination of Ngo Dinh Diem?
- Why had the Diem regime aroused so much opposition in South Vietnam?
- What were the consequences for the Vietnam conflict of Diem's assassination?

DOCUMENT STUDY

Did North Vietnam control the Viet Cong? The United States Department of State produced this paper in 1961:

" The Government and the Communist Party in North Viet-Nam provide support and encouragement to the illegal movement to destroy the Republic of Viet-Nam. The Communist Party, called the Lao Dong (Workers) Party in North Viet-Nam, provides the ideological orientation of the so-called 'liberation movement' in South Viet-Nam.

The following excerpts from Lao Dong Party declarations and from the articles and speeches of party and government officials in Hanoi demonstrate clearly the leading role played by North Viet-Nam in the Viet Cong campaign in the South:

1. From the resolution of the 3d National Congress of the Lao Dong (Workers) Party of Viet-Nam adopted at Hanoi on September 10, 1960:

'In the present stage, the Vietnamese revolution has two strategic tasks: first, to carry out the socialist revolution in North Viet-Nam; second, to liberate South Viet-Nam from the ruling yoke of the U.S. imperialists and their henchmen in order to achieve national unity and complete independence and freedom throughout the country. These two strategic tasks are closely related to each other and spur each other forward...

'The immediate task of the revolution in the South is to achieve the unity of the whole people, to fight resolutely against the aggressive and war-mongering U.S. imperialists, to overthrow the dictatorial Ngo Dinh Diem ruling clique, lackeys of the democratic coalition government in South Viet-Nam, to win national independence and establish democratic freedoms, to improve the people's livelihood, to safeguard peace, to achieve national reunification on the basis of independence and democracy, and to make an active contribution to the defense of peace in Southeast Asia and the world...

'To insure the complete success of the revolutionary struggle in South Viet-Nam our people there must strive to establish a united bloc of workers, peasants, and soldiers and to bring into being a broad national united front directed against the U.S.–Diem clique and based on the worker-peasant alliance. This front must rally all the patriotic classes and sections of the people, the majority and minority nationalities, all patriotic parties and religious groupings, together with all individuals inclined to oppose the U.S.–Diem clique. The aims of its struggle are peace, national independence, democratic freedoms, improvement of the people's living conditions, and peaceful national reunification.' ”

'A Threat to the Peace. North Vietnam's Effort to Conquer South Vietnam.' Part II. The Appendices. US Department of State. Bureau of Public Affairs. 1961

- What do you think was the purpose of the United States in publishing this document in 1961?
- The United States claims that North Vietnam was playing a 'leading role' in the Viet Cong campaign in the South. Does the Lao Dong resolution support this claim?
- What type of support was North Vietnam prepared to give the South?
- What was to be the purpose of the (National Liberation) Front? Was the Front to be a Communist organisation?

“ *The Do Luc Diary*

After a fight at Daktrum on September 3, 1961, forces of the Republic of Viet-Nam found a diary in the uniform of a Viet Cong soldier who had been killed in the engagement. Together with the diary were several pictures. One shows two men and a young boy. The men are wearing the uniform of the Army of North Viet-Nam...

'Suddenly, on December 15, 1960,...

'I answered the needs of the international solidarity of the Vietnamese-Laotian proletariat. I had to leave my beloved fatherland and my sweet life and go to help our friends with a spirit of unselfishness, of class solidarity, of love for my fatherland, and the spirit of the international proletarian revolution.

'For the third time my life turned to war again. For the liberation of our compatriots in the South, a situation of boiling oil and burning fire is necessary! A situation in which husband is separated from wife, father from son, brother from brother is necessary. I joined the ranks of the liberation army in answer to the call of the front for liberation of the South...

'Now my life is full of hardship — not enough rice to eat nor enough salt to give a taste to my tongue, not enough clothing to keep myself warm!

But in my heart I keep loyal to the Party and to the people. I am proud and happy.

'I am writing down this story for my sons and my grandsons of the future to know of my life and activities during the revolution when the best medicine available was the root of the wild banana tree and the best bandage was the leaf of ran lui, when there was no salt to give a taste to our meals, when there was no such food as meat or fish like we enjoy in a time of peace and happiness such as I have known and left behind. But that day will not take long to return to my life.' ”

'A Threat to the Peace', Appendix M

- Why would the US Department of State include this diary extract in its book?
- How typical do you think Do Luc's experiences were?

KEY EVENTS

1954 Geneva Conference divides Vietnam. Ngo Dinh Diem becomes prime minister.
1955 Diem crushes opposition and defeats Bao Dai in an arranged election to become president of the Republic of Vietnam.
1956 Diem cancels village elections.
1957 Viet Cong attacks develop; 400 assassinations.
1959 Diem's dictatorship tightens with increasing arrests of opponents.
1960 Attempt to overthrow Diem fails. National Liberation Front formed.
1961 Kennedy becomes president. Big gains for Viet Cong who now collect taxes in forty-one of the South's forty-four provinces. US supplies 700 military advisers.
1962 Strategic hamlet program runs into great opposition. US advisers now number 3000.
1963 US military advisers increased to 16 000. Buddhist protests begin in May. Diem overthrown and assassinated on 2 November. Kennedy assassinated 22 November.

JOHNSON GOES TO WAR

CHAPTER SIX

1964–1965

A GREAT AMOUNT of planning and thought went into the coup that removed Ngo Dinh Diem, but unfortunately neither the generals nor the Americans gave much thought to the type of government that would replace him. The generals' main worry became preserving their own positions, and keeping the armed forces unified. Those people amongst the plotters who had genuinely wanted change in Vietnam were pushed aside and replaced by insecure generals with no vision for the future. Their own plottings and personal intrigues became more important than the need to join together to save the country. Whilst the generals were playing musical chairs in Saigon, improvements in the lives of the peasants in the villages were impossible. The old officials continued to oppress the peasants, and the Viet Cong continued to increase its influence.

The assassination of John F. Kennedy three weeks after that of Ngo Dinh Diem threw American policy into further confusion. There was a feeling that the US had become too involved in Vietnamese politics, and that this had contributed to Diem's death. The US then went to the other extreme, and decided that it should not interfere. Unfortunately, this was one time when interference may have helped as the generals clearly lacked direction.

Ngo Dinh Diem was replaced by a military junta (group) of twelve called the Military Revolutionary Committee. There was no appointed leader of the committee, but its dominant figure was the 6-foot(1.8 metres)-tall General Duong Van Minh. 'Big Minh' was determined not to allow a dictatorship to re-emerge in Vietnam, but he did not offer any clear alternative. He managed to combine inefficiency with a lack of interest in the job, preferring to play tennis rather than rule.

General Khanh staged a second coup at the end of January 1964 to seize power from General Minh. Khanh had more energy and direction than Minh, which at first impressed the Americans. They expressed support for his government, and increased their aid. But the problems he faced were enormous. The morale of the people was low, and they had come to regard a Communist takeover as inevitable. The strategic hamlet program had collapsed, and the fortifications had been destroyed. Khanh's Government changed members seven times in the next twelve months. General Khanh could not inspire the Army to any victories. Instead, he planned to invade North Vietnam, but the Americans convinced him that this was ridiculous, given that he could not even control the countryside around Saigon. By mid-1964, the Viet Cong were launching attacks at positions only 10 kilometres from the centre of Saigon. Bomb attacks in Saigon were common. The sense of impending doom was captured by the American writer Robert Shaplen when he returned to Saigon shortly after Khanh had taken over:

> "We could almost feel the internal stresses and conflicts. The face of the town showed it. The prostitutes were more brazen, the beggars, including hordes of tattered youngsters with automatically outstretched hands, were more professional, and there was a sudden appearance of Vietnamese 'Teddy boys', who went out of their way to pick fights with American servicemen."

Shaplen, *The Lost Revolution*, p. 243

In early 1964, the North Vietnamese leaders decided that President Johnson would continue to support the South, and that they would therefore have to increase their support for the Viet Cong. They had fought the French, and they now realised that they would also have to fight the Americans. The Ho Chi Minh Trail at this stage was a very rough track hacked through the jungle for Viet Cong cadres to infiltrate south. The North now started to build up the trail, so that it eventually became almost a highway along which trucks could pass, protected from the air by the jungle canopy. From mid-1964, North Vietnamese troops also started to move down the trail to build up the Viet Cong forces, which had already reached 50 000.

Johnson's ideas on and approach to Vietnam were similar in a number of ways to those of Kennedy. Amongst them were:

- The belief that the United States could not withdraw as this would be interpreted worldwide as a sign of weakness.
- The view that all Communist countries were conspiring against the United States, without recognising that there were differences between them that could be exploited, e.g. the North Vietnamese suspicion of the Chinese.
- The lack of a clear *policy* on how to defeat Communism, and what would replace it. Rather, the US had a general idea that Communism was bad, and had an *ambition* to stop it.
- The attempt to defeat ideas (Communism, unity, nationalism, anti-imperialism) with weapons.

Johnson's major problem during 1964 was that he faced an election in November. He did not want to be seen to be using too much force in Vietnam, especially as he was trying to portray his Republican opponent, Barry Goldwater, as a warmonger. (Johnson at one stage told the generals that they could have their war after he was elected.) However, with the situation rapidly deteriorating in mid-1964, Johnson at least wanted to prepare the way for possible future action. He needed his Constitutional excuse, and he got it with the Gulf of Tonkin incident.

THE GULF OF TONKIN INCIDENT

The events leading up to the Gulf of Tonkin incident unfolded as follows:

Early June President Johnson's advisers secretly prepare a resolution to be put before the US Congress that would give approval for Johnson to go to war in Indo China.

30 July Four South Vietnamese patrol boats attack radar installations off the North Vietnamese coast.

2 August USS *Maddox*, cruising 12 to 15 kilometres off the North Vietnamese coast, is testing the effectiveness of the North's radar. Three North Vietnamese patrol boats attack, with one bullet hitting the *Maddox*. One of the North Vietnamese patrol boats is sunk and the other two damaged.

3 August Additional US bombers sent to Thailand and troops put on alert.

4 August The USS *Maddox* is ordered to zigzag off the North Vietnamese coast. In a thunderstorm, it reports that its radar shows it is under attack. Four hours later it reports that it may have been mistaken. None of the crew or the pilots overhead report any sightings.

5 August At 10.30 a.m. sixty-four US bombers take off. Half an hour later Johnson tells the people that he has ordered an attack because of 'renewed hostile actions against United States ships on the high seas in the Gulf of Tonkin'. The bombers attack ports and oil storage installations in North Vietnam, sinking twenty-five ships and destroying 10 per cent of oil supplies.

6 August The earlier resolution is presented to Congress and passed with only two senators opposing it. Opinion polls show that 85 per cent of Americans support Johnson's actions.

The Gulf of Tonkin Resolution

The Resolution gave the President power to 'take all necessary measures to repel any armed attack against the forces of the United States and to prevent further aggression... including the use of armed force, to assist any member... of the South East Asia Collective Defense Treaty'. It allowed Johnson a free hand to conduct the war in South East Asia as he saw fit, without having to come back to Congress for approval. Its passage by such a large majority removed Vietnam as an election issue.

The Resolution was extremely important to the future participation of the United States in Vietnam. It formed the basis of US involvement and represented full Congressional authority for military action in South East Asia. It gave Johnson a justification for later escalating the war. The Resolution had avoided the necessity for a declaration of war. It also was significant for another reason:

> “...the Administration had indeed lied to Congress regarding the details of the Tonkin affair, obscuring the political fact that the policy had been drawn up much earlier, and had predetermined its responses. Above all, the White House claimed it had been provoked when in reality it was the provoker.

> What was crucial about the Tonkin affair was the precedent of manipulation that it created for future administration relations with Congress and the public. ”

Kolko, *Vietnam*, p. 125

Johnson had misled Congress and the public and would need to continue to mislead them. President Nixon followed and expanded this pattern of presidential secrecy and cover-up, until it brought him to grief in the Watergate affair and seriously damaged the standing of the President in US politics.

Review

- Why would Johnson try and provoke the North? How did he do this?
- Why was the Gulf of Tonkin Resolution important to the future participation of the United States in Indo China?

Research

- What were OPLAN 34A and the De Soto Mission?

TURMOIL CONTINUES

If the Gulf of Tonkin Resolution was designed to strengthen Khanh's position then it failed. Street protests against his government developed during August. On 21 August the Buddhists joined in, demanding Khanh's resignation. He stepped aside on 25 August but the riots continued and 450 people were killed in street clashes involving Buddhists, Catholics and the troops. Khanh returned to power in early September only to face an attempted Army coup on 13 September. Somehow he survived until December when another round of coups developed. On 21 December US Ambassador Maxwell Taylor called Khanh, Ky and Thieu to his office and gave them a blunt lecture, blaming them for the mess that the country was now in.

In early February 1965 Ky and Thieu decided that Khanh's time had run out. Khanh escaped by plane to Dalat and, after a few days negotiating with Ky, decided to go overseas as an 'ambassador-at-large'. He was never to return. Ky later became Prime Minister and Thieu his Chief of State. One of Johnson's advisers, William Bundy, described them as 'the bottom of the barrel, absolutely the bottom of the barrel'.[1] Despite this, Ky was Prime Minister for the next two years, and Thieu took over until 1975.

Viet Cong provocation

The Viet Cong had been building up its strength through 1964, and by November had about 130 000 troops. It was also more clearly under the direction of North Vietnam. In a series of raids, the Viet Cong demonstrated its strength to the Americans. On 2 November it attacked the Bien Hoa US airbase just outside

The turmoil in South Vietnam brought to the fore Air Vice Marshal Nguyen Cao Ky, seen here with his wife touring the battlefield near Bong Sen. They often dressed in such outfits, trying to present a fashionable image (Photo by Nguyen Thanh Tai, UPI/Bettmann Newsphotos)

Saigon, destroying six aircraft and damaging another twenty. This was the first attack on a major US installation. A Christmas Eve attack on the Brinks Hotel in Saigon killed two Americans. A series of attacks was launched throughout South Vietnam, including one by two battalions on a village near Saigon. These were very heavy defeats for the ARVN (Army of the Republic of Vietnam), but they did not provoke a response from Johnson. However, retaliation came after an attack on the US base at Pleiku in early February 1965.

President Johnson's first act was to launch Operation Flaming Dart, an air attack on a North Vietnamese army camp. On 2 March he started Operation Rolling Thunder. This was to become a widespread bombing attack on the North that would continue for three years. President Johnson had clearly given up on a political solution — if he had ever really believed in one — and had decided that military force would do the job. The first Rolling Thunder attack was on an ammunition depot and involved 100 bombers. From May 1965 onwards US planes dropped an average of 800 tonnes of bombs a day on bridges, railways and military installations in the North.

Up to this point, the American troops in South Vietnam were still 'advisers'. The first combat troops, 3500 Marines, landed on the beach near Da Nang on 8 March. They were given the specific job of protecting the US Air Force bases, as requested by General Westmoreland. During April and May a further 72 000 troops were sent to Vietnam without too much publicity. Their role also was changed from one of defending the bases to what was called active defence, going out on patrols to find Viet Cong and kill them. The American people were not told of this important change of policy for several months.

The entry of United States combat troops also marked a significant change in relations between the US and the South Vietnamese Government. The US Ambassador, Maxwell Taylor, had advised against sending combat troops as he felt this might discourage the South Vietnamese from helping themselves. Johnson instead accepted the advice of his Field Commander, General William Westmoreland, and gave him what was really carte blanche to follow his own policy. Unfortunately, Westmoreland's policy was escalation, and his attitude was that any problem could be solved by sending more troops.

The South Vietnamese, who had not even asked for the troops to be sent, clearly became the minor partner. It now became easy for the Viet Cong to portray the Americans as invaders in Vietnam. The greater the United States presence became, the more the Vietnamese would look on them as imperialists. Instead of the war being a civil war against Communism, or a struggle between the North and the South for power, it became increasingly a war against foreign invasion. Johnson was advised repeatedly that he could not win such a war, but the 'hawks' amongst his advisers were more powerful at this stage than the 'doves'. One of the doves was Undersecretary of State George Ball, who wrote the following to Johnson in July.

Senator Fulbright (left) and President Johnson. Fulbright was chairman of the Senate Foreign Relations Committee that helped the President secure passage of the Gulf of Tonkin Resolution. Fulbright later became an outspoken opponent of the war (Lyndon B. Johnson Library)

Jeremy Barnes, *The Pictorial History of the Vietnam War*, Bison Books, London, 1988, p. 75

> The South Vietnamese are losing the war to the Viet Cong. No one can assure you that we can beat the Viet Cong, or even force them to the conference table on our terms, no matter how many hundred thousand (troops) we deploy.

Another adviser, J.T. McNaughton, was quite clear on what the aims of the United States were in entering the war:

Barnes, *Pictorial History of the Vietnam War*, p. 75

> 70 per cent — to avoid a humiliating United States defeat (to our reputation as a guarantor); 20 per cent — to keep SVN territory from Chinese hands; 10 per cent — to permit the people of SVN to enjoy a better, freer way of life.

Despite this advice, Westmoreland's escalation policy became the way to go for the United States up to the Tet Offensive in late January 1968. Numbers quickly built to 200 000 by the end of 1965, and to over half a million by the start of 1968.

LYNDON BAINES JOHNSON (LBJ)

Lyndon Johnson was a Texas school teacher who became one of the most powerful and effective politicians in Washington, a wheeler and dealer and a man who got things done. Kennedy chose him as his running mate for Vice President in 1960 to help his own chances of election as President, and to gain crucial votes in Texas. However, the two were from vastly different backgrounds and there was no close personal or working relationship between them. LBJ was largely disregarded by Kennedy, and the Eastern establishment circle around Kennedy looked down on him as a bit of a hick. During 1963, Johnson was not kept up to date on policy and rarely got to see Kennedy.

When John Kennedy was assassinated, Johnson took over suddenly as an unelected President, surrounded by Kennedy's advisers. He felt that he had to prove himself. His great ambition was to introduce wide-ranging social reforms to America, under the label of the Great Society. His great fear was that if he lost Vietnam he would lose the presidency. His Vietnam policy was designed to keep him popular so that he could introduce the Great Society. Johnson increasingly came to realise that he was trapped between the two:

> 'I knew from the start that I was bound to be crucified either way I moved. If I left the woman I really loved — the Great Society — in order to get involved with that bitch of a war on the other side of the world, then I would lose everything at home. All my programs… But if I left that war and let the Communists take over South Vietnam, then I would be seen as a coward and my nation would be seen as an appeaser.'

Doris Kearns, *Lyndon Johnson and the American Dream*, Harper & Row, New York, 1976, as quoted in Karnow, *Vietnam*, p. 320

Review

- In what ways had there been a political collapse in South Vietnam by early 1965?
- What changes were there in the military situation by February 1965?
- Why did Johnson decide to start the Rolling Thunder operation? Why did he send combat troops?
- Why did Johnson reject the advice that the United States could not win?
- Why did the number of US troops escalate so quickly after the first landing on 8 May?

Discuss

- What were the hawks and the doves? Who was in each group?
- How did the sending of combat troops change the relationship between the United States and the South Vietnamese?
- Which groups in South Vietnam would have seen the entry of the Americans as a foreign invasion?

Research

Find out about the background, personality and careers of Nguyen Cao Ky and Nguyen Van Thieu.

Structured questions

- Why didn't the assassination of Diem improve the situation in Vietnam?
- Why did the North Vietnamese Government decide to increase support for the Viet Cong in early 1964? What type of support did they give?
- How did this increase the involvement of the United States in Vietnam?

DOCUMENT STUDY

Who was the aggressor?

A Pattern for Peace in Southeast Asia: the Johns Hopkins Speech by Lyndon B. Johnson

“The world as it is in Asia is not a serene or peaceful place. The first reality is that North Vietnam has attacked the independent nation of South Vietnam. Its object is total conquest.

Of course, some of the people of South Vietnam are participating in this attack on their own government. But trained men and supplies, orders and arms, flow in a constant stream from North to South.

This support is the heartbeat of the war.

And it is a war of unparalleled brutality. Simple farmers are the targets of assassination and kidnapping. Women and children are strangled in the night because their men are loyal to their Government. Small and helpless villages are ravaged by sneak attacks. Large-scale raids are conducted on towns, and terror strikes in the heart of cities.

The confused nature of this conflict cannot mask the fact that it is the new face of an old enemy. It is an attack by one country upon another. And the object of that attack is a friend to which we are pledged.

Over this war, and all Asia, is another reality: the deepening shadow

Selections from *Department of State Bulletin*, LII, 26 April 1965, pp. 606–10

of Communist China. The rulers in Hanoi are urged on by Peking. This is a regime which has destroyed freedom in Tibet, attacked India, and been condemned by the United Nations for aggression in Korea. It is a nation which is helping the forces of violence in almost every continent. The contest in Vietnam is part of a wider pattern of aggressive purpose. ”

Militancy of the National Liberation Front (March 1965)

“ For more than ten years now, the U.S. imperialists have continuously interfered in and committed aggression against South Vietnam. Of late, they have brought into South Vietnam many more units of U.S. combat troops composed of missile units, marines, B-57 strategic bombers, together with mercenary troops from South Korea, Taiwan, the Philippines, Australia, Malaya, etc. They even frenziedly ordered the air forces of the U.S.A. and its henchmen to conduct repeated air raids on North Vietnam and Laos. At present, not only are they stubbornly stepping up their criminal aggressive war in South Vietnam but are also attempting to fan up the flames of war throughout Indochina and Southeast Asia.

The puppet administration, hangers-on of the U.S.A., in South Vietnam is daily committing more heinous crimes against the country. The impudent traitors are kowtowing before the aggressors and are bringing in snakes to kill chickens of the home coop, inviting troops of the United States and many of its satellite countries to come to South Vietnam to massacre our people, occupy and trample upon the territory of our sacred fatherland, and oppress and exploit our people most harshly. ”

Statement of the Central Committee of the South Vietnam National Liberation Front, 22 March 1965, in *Vietnam Courier: Information and Documents* [Hanoi], No.23, 3 April 1965

- What is President Johnson's aim in his speech?
- What are the main points in Johnson's speech that the National Liberation Front would not agree with?
- Look closely at the type of language used in the NLF statement. Who would be influenced by it? How does it influence your assessment of this source as historical evidence?

US thoughts on the Viet Cong

Secretary of State (1962)

“ The guerrillas whom the Vietnamese Army are fighting are under distinct handicaps. In many cases they are poorly trained and equipped and not motivated by deep conviction. Rather, they are merely unsophisticated villagers or peasants who have been conscripted by terror or treachery. In such a case they are likely to have had only rudimentary training in weapons-handling and tactics. Their equipment may be makeshift, often just what they can capture or fabricate themselves.

Only the leaders and the hard core have a strong ideological commitment. The rank and file are their puppets — those whom they have bought, coerced, or intimidated. ”

US Under-Secretary of State, George W. Ball, *Vietnam: Free-World Challenge in Southeast Asia*, Department of State Publication 7388: Far Eastern Series 113, Washington, DC, 1962, p. 15

United States Government 'White Paper' (February 1965)

" South Vietnam is fighting for its life against a brutal campaign of terror and armed attack inspired, directed, supplied, and controlled by the Communist regime in Hanoi. This flagrant aggression has been going on for years, but recently the pace has quickened and the threat has now become active...

This report is a summary of the massive evidence of North Vietnamese aggression obtained by the Government of South Vietnam. This evidence has been jointly analyzed by South Vietnamese and American experts.

The evidence shows that the hard core of the Communist forces attacking South Vietnam were trained in the North and ordered into the South by Hanoi. It shows that the key leadership of the Vietcong (VC), the officers and much of the cadre, many of the technicians, political organizers, and propagandists have come from the North and operate under Hanoi's direction. It shows that the training of essential military personnel and their infiltration into the South is directed by the Military High Command in Hanoi.

The evidence shows that many of the weapons and much of the ammunition and other supplies used by the Vietcong have been sent into South Vietnam from Hanoi. In recent months new types of weapons have been introduced in the VC army, for which all ammunition must come from outside sources. Communist China and other Communist states have been the prime suppliers of these weapons and ammunition, and they have been channeled primarily through North Vietnam. "

Aggression from the North: The Record of North Vietnam's Campaign to Conquer South Vietnam, Department of State Publication 7839, Far Eastern Series 130, Washington, D.C., 1965

- Compare the two views of the Viet Cong. In what ways are they different?
- Is one view more accurate than the other?
- Who has changed between 1962 and 1965: the Americans or the Viet Cong?

'ALL THE WAY WITH LBJ'

CHAPTER SEVEN

FOR OVER 100 YEARS, Australians feared invasion by Asians from the North. This xenophobia became popularly known as the 'Yellow Peril', and led to the development of the White Australia policy at the turn of the century. World War II seemed to give reality to this fear, as the Japanese bombed Darwin, took over most of New Guinea, and even sent midget submarines into Sydney Harbour. After the war, Australia added the 'Red Menace' to the Yellow Peril as one of its phobias. Fear of Communism became a consuming national passion. World War II also made Australia very aware of its small population and its isolation as a European settlement in Asia. Australians still saw themselves as Europeans, and gave no thought to accepting Asians as equals. Politics was dominated from 1949 by the conservative Robert Menzies, who exploited these fears of Communists and Asians to keep winning re-election. For Menzies, Asia was an area one flew over on the way to England to visit the Queen or watch the cricket.

The only way Australians could protect themselves in this potentially hostile environment was to have a powerful friend, and until 1941, Britain had filled this role. When Britain became too absorbed in its own problems, Australia turned to the United States for help against Japan. After the war, Australia wanted to retain the United States as its protector, and tried to manoeuvre it into an alliance and into setting up bases in Australia. The Korean War pushed the United States into accepting the alliances, which have been seen as Australia's protection since then.

The two main agreements of importance to Australia were:

ANZUS Agreement 1951: Australia, New Zealand, United States. They agreed to assist one another in case of attack.

Article III: The parties will consult together whenever in the opinion of any one of them the territorial integrity, political independence or security of any of the parties is threatened in the Pacific.

SEATO 1954 (South East Asia Collective Defence Treaty): USA, Britain, France, Australia, New Zealand, Thailand, Pakistan. They placed South Vietnam, Laos and Cambodia under their protection. They agreed to meet together if there was an armed attack on one of them and, if agreement was unanimous, to take action 'at the invitation or with the consent of the government concerned'.

Review

Under what conditions of the SEATO treaty would Australia be obliged to fight in Vietnam?

INVOLVING UNCLE SAM

Conservative Australian politicians felt that although these alliances were strong, security could only be guaranteed if the United States was actively involved in Asia. A report commissioned by Prime Minister Gough Whitlam in 1975 outlined the reasons for Australia's involvement in Vietnam:

> "The provision of military aid by Australia was decided upon for political reasons and was in support of the fundamental aim of Australian policy towards South Vietnam, which was to ensure the long term defence interests of Australia. These were seen in terms of the ANZUS and SEATO Treaties and the theory of forward defence against the victory of communism in South-East Asia, an area seen as vital to Australia's future. This was a policy developed in Australia independently of any outside pressure. The corner-stone of this policy was seen as a compelling necessity to commit the power of the United States to the Asian area and thus to commit her to a tactical guarantee of active support to Australia through the ANZUS and SEATO Treaties."

'Australia's Military Commitment to Vietnam', Canberra, May 1975, p.23, quoted in Frank Frost, *Australia's War in Vietnam*, Allen & Unwin, Sydney, 1987

The problem of maintaining United States involvement in Australia's near north became more serious as the situation in Indonesia developed. By 1962 the Indonesians had used pressure to take over West Irian from the Dutch. Australia tried to prevent this but received no support from the Americans. During 1964 Australia's relations with Indonesia deteriorated as Sukarno's rule became increasingly erratic. Communist influence was growing and Sukarno was cultivating relations with Communist China. In early 1965 Australia faced the prospect of having a neighbour on the New Guinea border that might become Communist, with no firm guarantee of United States protection. Greg Lockhart points out that Australia's aim then 'was to do everything possible to draw American power into the region. This included both encouragement and support for American involvement in the Vietnam War.'[1]

Australia's ambassador to the United States explained in 1964 that this could be done without excessive cost.

> Our objective should be, it is suggested, to achieve such an habitual closeness of relations with the United States and sense of mutual alliance that in our time of need... the United States would have little option but to respond as we would want.
>
> The problem of Vietnam is one, it seems, where we could without a disproportionate expenditure pick up a lot of credit with the United States for this problem is one to which the United States is deeply committed and in which it genuinely feels it is carrying too much of the load.

Michael Sexton, *War for the Asking*, Penguin, Melbourne, 1981, pp. 44–5

Review

Why was Australia encouraging United States involvement in Vietnam? Was Australia taking advantage of the Americans' commitment to Vietnam?

The size of the Australian Army had decreased by the early 1960s. With potential problems in Indonesia and Vietnam, the Australian Government decided it was time to build it up again rapidly by introducing conscription in November 1964. Three months' military service had been compulsory for all 18-year-olds until the mid-1950s, but the Army was now recommending two years at age 20. However, the Army did not need the number of men

"That's Carmichael our commitment to Malaysia, Shadbolt our commitment to Borneo, O'Toole our commitment to Vietnam and Gribble our defence of the mainland."

Les Tanner, the Bulletin *1964, courtesy of Les Tanner*

a draft of all 20-year-olds would produce. It was now proposed that all eligible men must register and a certain number of birthdates would be drawn from a barrel in a twice yearly conscription 'lottery'. This meant that some men would be required to give two years to national service while others would be free to pursue their lives and develop careers.

- What point is the cartoon on page 75 making about Australia's armed forces?

THE DECISION

Australia had sent thirty military advisers to South Vietnam in 1962, and this number had risen to a hundred by early 1965. In March 1965, when the United States sent combat troops, Australia saw the opportunity of gaining favour with the Americans by increasing its involvement. The United States was very happy to have support from other countries so that it would not look as if it was acting alone. The US even later paid the costs of Korean and Filipino troops fighting in Vietnam.

In December 1964, President Johnson asked Australia to increase its number of advisers. Australia replied that it could not send any more advisers, as these were specially trained soldiers, but it offered to send a combat battalion. Because the United States did not have any combat troops in Vietnam at this stage, it did not accept Australia's offer. But with rapid US build-up, starting in March 1965, the Americans, on 13 April, decided to accept the Australian offer of a battalion. Menzies planned to announce this in Parliament on 29 April. The only problem was how to get the South Vietnamese Government to request the battalion, as it was already worried that the increasing United States presence was threatening its independence and weakening its ability to counter Viet Cong propaganda. The only clear ideology it could present to the Vietnamese people was that it was strongly nationalist. By allowing foreigners to take over the country, that policy would be seen to have failed and the Viet Cong would increasingly look like the only alternative.

By 22 April, the United States and Australia had agreed on what role the battalion would play. It was proposed to base the men at Vung Tau and to use them for Search and Destroy missions, of the active defence kind that the United States had started around their Bien Hoa base. But still they had not asked the South Vietnamese Government.

On 26 April, the Australian ambassador to the United States, Keith Waller, sent a message to Canberra, explaining that although the Americans were putting some pressure on Prime Minister Quat, he had still not agreed.

> “Accordingly, while fully understanding your wish to make an early announcement, the Americans cannot at this time say whether the prerequisite of Quat's agreement to the establishment of the new enclaves

Sexton, *War for the Asking*, p. 162

and to the dispatch of the Australian battalion will or will not be satisfied by Thursday night Australian time. ”

News of the expected announcement was leaked to the newspapers, and appeared on the morning of 29 April. Still there was no word from Saigon. During the afternoon, Prime Minister Menzies received a letter from President Johnson congratulating him on his decision. At 5.10 p.m. that day, the Australian ambassador in Saigon cabled that he had received a message from Prime Minister Quat welcoming the Australian offer. This was enough for Menzies, and he proceeded to announce Australia's involvement in Parliament at 8.00 p.m. Later that night, Quat finally sent a letter to the Australian ambassador.

“ 29th April, 1965

The Honorable
H.D. Anderson
Ambassador of the Government of Australia
Saigon, Vietnam.

Dear Mr. Ambassador,

I have the honor to refer to your letter of today's date confirming the Australian Government's offer to send to Viet Nam an infantry battalion of 800 men, with some 100 personnel in logistic support to serve with United States forces in assisting in the defence of the Republic of Vietnam.

I wish to confirm my government's acceptance of this offer and to request the dispatch of this force to Viet Nam on the basis which we discussed.

Sincerely,
PHAN-HUY-QUAT ”

Sexton, *War for the Asking*, p. 172

AUSTRALIA HONOURS TREATY
Troops to protect South Vietnamese

CANBERRA, Thurs.: Australia would send an infantry battalion against the Viet Cong in South Vietnam, the Prime Minister, Sir Robert Menzies, announced tonight.

The men of the first Battalion, Royal Australian Regiment, now based at Holsworth, in N.S.W., will be sent to the area.

But their departure and deployment is secret — this being worked out in conjunction with the South Vietnamese and United States authorities.

When the first Battalion troops leave Australia for South Vietnam they will become the first formation Australia has deployed for combat under S.E.A.T.O.

They will also become the first Australian formation to go overseas since World War II for combat duties outside of a British Commonwealth operation (Malaysia) or a United Nations effort (Korea).

REQUESTED

Sir Robert told the House of Representatives tonight that the decision to send the troops had been made after a request from South Vietnam and close consultations with the United States.

Both sides of the packed house were silent as Sir Robert said: "The task of holding the situation in South Vietnam and restraining the North Vietnamese is formidable.

"The takeover of South Vietnam would be a direct military threat for Australia and all the countries of South and South-East Asia. It must be seen as part of a thrust by Communist China between the Indian and Pacific Oceans."

DELIGHTED

President Johnson has welcomed the move. In a letter to the Prime Minister, he said: "I am delighted at the decision of your Government to provide an infantry battalion for service in South Vietnam at the request of the Government of South Vietnam."

The Labor Party is anxious to debate the Government's decision.

In the only official comment, the Leader of the Opposition, Mr. Calwell said: "The Federal Labor Party will consider the Prime Minister's statement and its implications at a meeting on Tuesday.

"I insist that the debate begin immediately after question time on Tuesday," he said.

Border Morning Mail, 30 April, 1965

Review

- Why was it important for Australia to receive a request from the South Vietnamese? Was it received?
- Quat's letter was not made public for six years. Why?
- What evidence is there that Menzies believed in the domino theory?
- What were Menzies' real reasons for sending troops?
- Why did the Labor Party leader, Arthur Calwell, not reply immediately?

The Team

The first Australian troops to go to Vietnam had been the thirty members of the Australian Army Training Team, known as the Team, who had been sent in July 1962 as military advisers. The size of the Team rose to a hundred by 1965 and stayed at about that level until 1972, when the Team became the last Australian soldiers to be withdrawn from Vietnam. The total number to serve with the Team was almost a thousand, and members earned four Victoria Crosses and many other decorations.

Isolation was one of the main problems that these advisers faced. Mostly they served in a South Vietnamese Army Unit with only one other Australian or American adviser. The average Australian adviser was 35 years old and was a specially selected officer or warrant officer. Their training often did not prepare them for dealing with the Vietnamese or with the Americans. Few advisers spoke Vietnamese when they arrived and most of them came to realise the great difficulty of giving advice through an interpreter. They found that their advice was more likely to be accepted if they gained the respect of the Vietnamese by accepting their customs, food and conditions.

A number of advisers were attached to Montagnard units. The Montagnards were mountain tribes from the Central Highlands who were racially different from the Vietnamese, and who distrusted them. Barry Petersen was an Australian adviser who spent two years with the Montagnards and built up a force of 1000 soldiers. Petersen learnt their language and adapted to their customs. When the South Vietnamese became worried that Petersen's army might threaten their authority, he was forced to leave the country.

The 1st Battalion

The 1st Battalion of the Royal Australian Regiment travelled to Vietnam on the aircraft carrier HMAS *Sydney*, and was established there by June 1965. It was attached first to the American Army (173rd Airborne Brigade) to carry out active defence of the air base at Bien Hoa. During the rest of 1965, the battalion helped the Americans in clearing operations in two areas near Saigon,

Barry Petersen in the traditional dress of the Montagnards with one of the Montagnard people and an Australian adviser (Australian War Memorial negative no. DNE/65/428/VN)

War Zone D and the Iron Triangle.[2] Both operations were declared highly successful by the Americans, but this meant only that the Viet Cong disappeared when the Americans approached and reappeared afterwards. The 1st Battalion undertook a number of Search and Destroy missions in early 1966. When they returned to Sydney in June, 26 had been killed and 114 wounded. Unlike later battalions, they were welcomed back by a crowd of 300 000.

THE TASK FORCE

The 1st Battalion was replaced by the Australian Task Force, consisting at first of the 5th and 6th Battalions. They were given responsibility for the province of Phuoc Tuy. The Task Force contained the first national servicemen to land in Vietnam and Private Errol Noack, on 24 May, became the first conscript in Australia's history to be killed overseas. The Task Force set up its permanent base at Nui Dat, 25 kilometres inland from its support base on the coast at Vung Tau. It remained there until it was withdrawn in 1971.

Phuoc Tuy was selected for the Australians because it gave them a readily identifiable area that would suit their training and the experience they had gained in places like Malaya. The province was about 60 kilometres by 30 kilometres, with a population of 100 000. There were several large groups of hills which had been bases for both the Viet Minh and the Viet Cong. The Long Hai Hills were riddled with caves and had been an excellent base for the guerrillas. Phuoc Tuy had been controlled by the Viet Minh during

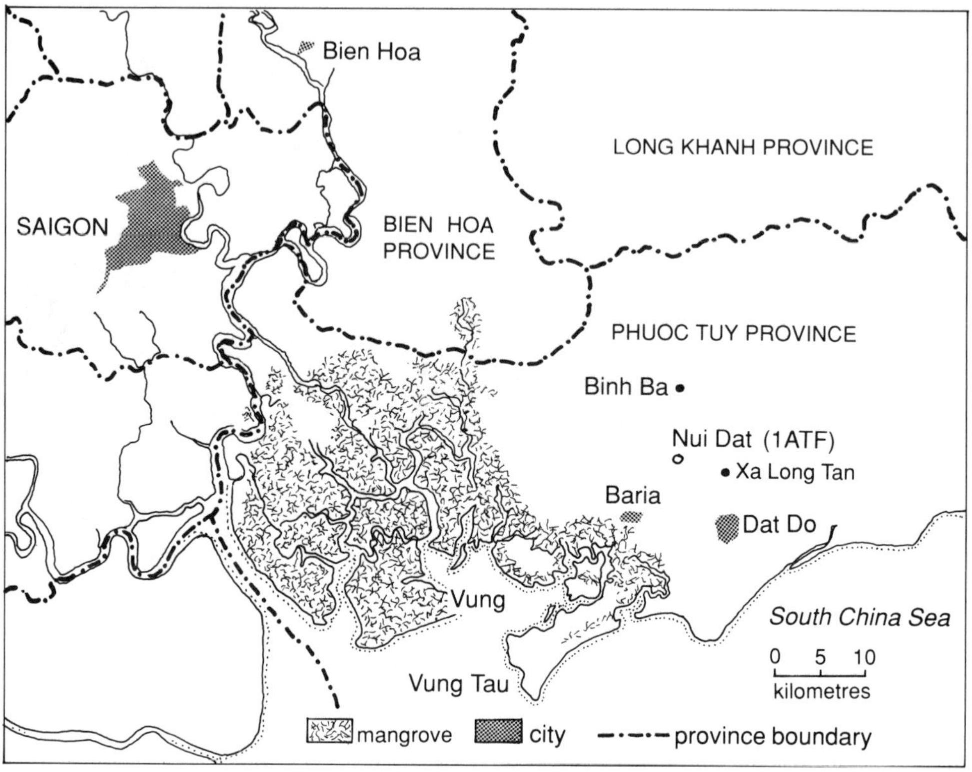

The Australian Task Force was given responsibility for the province of Phuoc Tuy. It was chosen because the conditions there suited the Australians' experience and training

the French War, and the Viet Cong had resumed activities there in 1959. By 1966, they were well established both politically and militarily, and had an estimated 7000 men in main force battalions, with 1000 more available as guerrilla fighters.

The first job for the Task Force was pacification of the province. The Australians started by clearing the Vietnamese villagers out of an area within 4000 metres, or mortar range, of the Nui Dat base. Cordon and search tactics were used to extend their control, and to cut off Viet Cong influence from the villages. By mid-August, the road from the provincial capital of Baria to the villages in the north was reopened.

DOCUMENT STUDY

Operation Enoggera

“Operation ENOGGERA was conducted between the 21st June, 1966, and the 5th July, 1966. This was the first Battalion operation. It was also a first for the First Australian Task Force, being an operation undertaken solely by us in Vietnam.

Our task was to search the village of Long Phuoc, about 2000 metres southwest of the Task Force Base, clear it of any Viet Cong and confiscate any caches of materials found. The destruction of any tunnels and caches and, in fact, the entire village, was also to be implemented.

The villagers of Long Phuoc had been resettled in Hoa Long before the operation began. The clearance of a village of this size and complexity had not previously been attempted by an Australian Force. The area was divided into sectors and companies given the responsibility of searching through them. Long Phuoc had been a well-established village with brick houses and many cultivated areas bounded by hedgerows.

The Armoured Personnel Carriers and the helicopters of 9 Sqn RAAF support the Battalion by backloading the rice and other materials found, apart from resupplying the troops in the field.

The enemy met were only small groups of local forces. Contacts were made with snipers and groups of up to four men.

Some months after the operation the Government of the Republic of South Vietnam gazetted that Long Phuoc no longer existed, and its name was removed from the official record of existing communities.

Losses

Enemy — 4 killed in action.
Own — 1 wounded in action.

Finds

49 tons of rice — 15 tunnels — 9 tons of salt — 11 weapons — medical supplies — documents — clothing — ammunition and explosives — panji stakes. ”

Captain I.M. Williams, *Vietnam, A Pictorial History of the Sixth Battalion, The Royal Australian Regiment*, Printcraft Press, 1967

“ We went on an operation called Operation Enoggera, to search and destroy the village of Long Phuoc, and when I say destroy I mean f — destroy. It's one of the things that's stuck in my craw all these years because Long Phuoc wasn't a little grass-hut village, Long Phuoc was a town.

The houses were on fairly large plots of land, probably half an acre to two acres. The houses were beautifully solid, set on concrete bases with tiled floors and big ceramic gables, and beautiful fruit trees and everything around. Wells were brick-sided, and a lot of the community sheds for rice storage were really large and beautifully mortared together, with timber. The roads were brick-paved roads.

We just absolutely destroyed the whole bloody lot. We pulled it to the ground and burnt it and blew it up. There was absolutely nothing left of Long Phuoc when we left, absolutely nothing.

I can remember pulling down this beautiful great big shed: we just piled it all together and set a match to it and burnt it. Anything that we couldn't pull down we got the engineers in and blew it up.

The people were resettled at Hoa Long, but they were resettled in shanties compared to what they had. ”

Interview with Terry Burstall in Stuart Rintoul, *Ashes of Vietnam*, Heinemann, Melbourne, 1987

- On what points do these accounts agree and disagree?
- What is the tone of these two accounts? Does the tone reveal the authors' attitudes towards the war?
- What attitudes do they both show towards the Vietnamese?
- As the first task force operation, should this be seen as a success?
- How would it have been reported in Australia at the time?

Cordon and search

This strategy was designed to eliminate Viet Cong influence from the villages. Before dawn, Australian troops would surround a village with a cordon of men. Helped by South Vietnamese soldiers, they would search the village for Viet Cong guerrillas and political leaders, as well as for arms and food stores. The entire population would be interrogated.

Long Tan

The Viet Cong felt that the Australians were rapidly gaining the upper hand, and that they needed to respond. They prepared for a large operation against the Task Force at Nui Dat. After clearing the area around Nui Dat, the Australians started to send patrols on sweeps through the nearby jungle. One of these patrols made contact with the 275th Regiment of the Viet Cong (People's Army of Vietnam) at 4.00 p.m. on 18 August in a rubber plantation near Long Tan, 5 kilometres from Nui Dat. A Viet Cong force of 2500 pinned 108 Australians down in pouring rain for the next three hours. Very accurate artillery fire from a New Zealand battery attached to the Task Force held the Viet Cong down and caused very severe casualties. A relieving company of Australians arrived at 7.00 p.m. Eighteen Australians were killed and 21 wounded; an estimated 245 Viet Cong were killed.

The Battle of Long Tan was the only major battle that the Australians were involved in during the war. It ensured that the Viet Cong were not able to operate in Phuoc Tuy province in anything like battalion strength afterwards.

Australian Nurse Ahern with a Vietnamese baby, part of the 'hearts and minds' strategy employed by both the Australians and the Americans (Australian War Memorial negative no. GIL/67/483/VN)

Civic action

Civic action activities were started in 1965 by the 1st Royal Australian Regiment. The 1st Australian Civil Affairs unit was formed in mid-1967. The aim of civic action was to win over the 'hearts and minds' of the people to the South Vietnamese Government. Projects included the building of schools, houses, hospitals, dispensaries, bridges, roads, water supplies, youth clubs and community centres. Medical and dental officers made weekly visits to villages. Advice was given to farmers. The soldiers were encouraged to help this work by trying to understand the people and their customs, and by treating the Vietnamese with respect and courtesy.

Review

- What was the role of the Australian Task Force in Phuoc Tuy province?
- How did the Task Force gain military control of the province?
- What difficulties would the Australians have had in gaining the hearts and minds of the people?

An Australian soldier crossing a creek. Conditions like this were commonplace in Vietnam (Australian War Memorial negative no. BUL/69/27/VN)

Patrols

Patrols were a constant activity for the soldiers, and were necessary to keep the area around the Nui Dat base clear of Viet Cong. Night ambush patrols would set out late in the afternoon, in the wet season usually in torrential rain that would soak the men very quickly.

> " In this condition they would squelch their way across country ensuring that they were not seen or heard, and at last light move into position. Throughout the night they would lie in their wet clothes trying to ignore the leeches attempting to extract their dues, waiting for the enemy. In the dry season they would lie sweating throughout the night, thirsty and dusty, trying not to think of the abundance of snakes in the area. In most cases the day patrolling was so effective that there would be no enemy in the area and most night ambushes went unsprung… It was a soul-destroying job. A job which had to be done as it was vital for the safety of everyone in the Task Force Area. "

Williams, *Vietnam, A Pictorial History*, p. 85

Search and Destroy

The Task Force carried out a number of Search and Destroy missions in Phuoc Tuy. The aim of these was to try to attack Viet Cong bases, usually in the hills, destroy the bases and capture weapons and food. If the Australians were fortunate, they might ambush some Viet Cong along one of the trails.

NVA soldiers captured by Australian forces (Australian War Memorial negative no. CRO/68/575/VN)

A typical operation was Operation Ingham, carried out by the Sixth Battalion in November 1966, with the aim of destroying the base of the Viet Cong Battalion D445.[3] The Sixth Battalion was moved by armoured personnel carrier (APC) from Nui Dat to the edge of a rubber plantation, and then marched 7 kilometres east. Over the next few days, the soldiers made contact with a few Viet Cong, but Battalion D445 had faded into the jungle, leaving behind just a few men to slow down the Australians. For the next two weeks, the Australians searched the area, supported by the APCs and helicopters. Many camps were found and destroyed before the Australians withdrew.

The Final Count

Viet Cong Losses	*Australian Losses*	*Australian Gains*
10 killed 10 wounded 1 taken prisoner 19 detained for interrogation	2 killed 22 wounded	85 tonnes of rice seized 27 Viet Cong camps destroyed Many documents and maps discovered

The minefield

The Task Force made a major mistake in laying a minefield from Dat Do to the coast. The field stretched for 10 kilometres and 20 000 anti-personnel mines were laid. The ARVN were supposed to patrol the minefield, but they failed to stop the Viet Cong from helping themselves to the mines. The Viet Cong relaid these mines in areas where the Australians would patrol, causing severe casualties.

The Air Force

The RAAF played an important supporting role. Helicopters were an integral part of the jungle war, particularly for dropping troops in, 'dusting off' the wounded, and as gunships supporting missions. Hercules aircraft were used to transport supplies and some soldiers to Vietnam, and for bringing the wounded home. Within Vietnam, Caribou aircraft were used for troop transport and cargo. Two squadrons of Canberra bombers flew missions over large areas of South Vietnam from 1967 to 1971. They were particularly useful in low-level, daylight attacks.

The Navy

Four Australian destroyers took part in the war, patrolling close to the coast of South Vietnam to give gunfire support to ground troops if required. They also worked with the US Navy in setting up a blockade off the coast of North Vietnam to stop them sending supplies by boat to Viet Cong in the South. Quite often, the North Vietnamese returned fire. Naval divers were used to keep Vung Tau harbour clear of sabotage charges. The Navy also supplied helicopter pilots and groundcrew to work with American units. Five pilots were killed in these operations.

Recreation

The most common form of relaxation for the troops was drinking beer. Each company in the Task Force had its own canteen, and with cans at 15 cents each plenty were consumed. Marijuana and heroin use was rare amongst the Australians, though much more frequent amongst the American soldiers. Alcohol-related accidents occurred, and there was one reported case of death

Australian troops board a US Chinook helicopter in Phuoc Tuy province (Australian War Memorial negative no. FAI/70/223/VN)

from alcoholic poisoning. Concerts were organised at Nui Dat, with artists flown out from Australia to entertain the troops. The first rock concert, with Col Joye and Little Pattie, was held on the night of the Battle of Long Tan.

Troops could get in-country leave for up to five days at Vung Tau. This had been a beach resort for the French and still had plenty of bars and restaurants. American-organised R & R (Rest and Recuperation) leave was available for the Australians, giving them five days in Bangkok, Hong Kong, Singapore or Taipeh.

Australian efforts at pacifying Phuoc Tuy impressed the American commander, General Westmoreland, who requested that these troops be moved to another area so that they could repeat their work. The Australians felt that this would endanger the progress they had made so far, but agreed to allowing their troops to be used outside the province. When the Viet Cong launched their Tet Offensive on 31 January 1968, two of the Task Force's three battalions were on operations with the Americans 50 kilometres away in Bien Hoa. About 600 Viet Cong from Battalion D445 attacked five positions in Baria, capital of Phuoc Tuy. Swift action by A Company of the 3rd Battalion, who were rushed to Baria in APCs, forced the Viet Cong to withdraw to Long Dien. An ARVN battalion made a weak attempt to remove them, but this was only achieved after D Company 3rd Battalion moved in to help. After eight days fighting, the Viet Cong withdrew and staged no more major attacks during 1968 in Phuoc Tuy. Although the Viet Cong were defeated and sustained heavy casualties, Tet had shown that they could still operate in force and that the province was not fully under government control. It also showed the weakness of the ARVN.

With Phuoc Tuy being of less importance during 1968, the Task Force was used on three separate occasions to help the Americans by protecting major US bases at Bien Hoa and Long Binh. From March 1969, the Task Force was consolidated in Phuoc Tuy and resumed the job of pacifying the province. The situation had altered, however, as North Vietnamese soldiers were increasingly replacing the Viet Cong. Bases in the hills had also been re-established. The stories of two villages show the problems that the Australians faced.

Sweet Water

> “I once watched a whole village of Vietnamese being transported to a makeshift settlement of tarred paper and shacks. I knew the area they came from. On the Viet Cong maps it was called Slope 30. It had always been Viet Minh and then Viet Cong. On the day the new makeshift village was opened, within artillery range of the Task Force at Nui Dat, I stood in the crowd. I had an ammunition pouch high up on my webbing and inside it a tape recorder. I had intended to listen to the Vietnamese and then

have it translated back in Saigon. Suddenly a Vietnamese standing beside me said something to the headman who was to take over the village.

I knew enough Vietnamese to make out the words. But I still took the tape back to Saigon to have it translated. I did not approve of the village which they called in Vietnamese, Sweet Water. I knew that where the Vietnamese had come from, there were the graves of their ancestors. I had been to Slope 30 with the Airborne and with the Australians. It was a pleasant village and we had uprooted the Vietnamese and taken them to an arid place far away from their pleasant cottages and the graves of their ancestors. What the Vietnamese near me had said to the new headman was, 'One night we will come in and cut your throat'. They did, too, a week later. ”

Australian journalist Pat Burgess, 'A correspondent's report' in Kenneth Maddock & Barry Wright, (eds) *War: Australia and Vietnam*, Harper & Row, Sydney, 1987

Binh Ba

The Australian troops rarely became involved in attacks on villages, but they were forced to in June 1969 when a force of largely North Vietnamese troops quietly moved into the village of Binh Ba. An Australian tank and armoured vehicle were fired on as they passed through the village. The Australians quickly had the village surrounded and trapped the Communists. They waited while ARVN officials tried to have the village evacuated, then they attacked, taking the village house by house. Fighting continued until the next day and the village was largely destroyed. More than sixty Vietnamese, and one Australian, were killed.

Review

- As an Australian soldier involved at Binh Ba, write back home to your younger brother telling him about your life in Vietnam, and giving him your thoughts on the progress of the war and on the ARVN and Viet Cong.
- What would the Viet Cong gain from firing on the Australian tank in Binh Ba?
- Would Operation Ingham have been considered a success?
- What was meant by pacification? Would the military tactics used by the Task Force have helped to pacify the province?

Discuss

- Brigadier Ted Serong, leader of the Australian Army Training Team, has said that the involvement of Australia in Vietnam was political. Was he correct? If so, how would this affect the performance of the Task Force?
- Stanley Karnow's book, *Vietnam: A History*, does not include any reference to Australia in the index. Is this typical of the American attitude to Australia's involvement?
- There were no official war photographers sent to Vietnam by Australia. Photos in the Australian War Memorial were mostly taken by Army public relations officials. What does this indicate?

AUSTRALIANS IN VIETNAM

The average Australian soldier was much better trained for the job than his American counterpart. All Australians had twelve months Army training before they were sent to Vietnam, and this included special jungle training at Canungra in Queensland. Many Americans were sent out after only a few months in the Army, and none were given jungle training. The Australians were sent out for twelve months with their battalion or brigade and stayed with that unit, building up a valuable team spirit. The American was sent out for a personal tour of duty of twelve months. The American commander, General Westmoreland, valued the Australians.

Frost, *Australia's War in Vietnam*, p. 78

> “Small in number and well-trained, particularly in anti-guerrilla warfare, the Australian Army was much like the post-Versailles German Army in which even men in the ranks might have been leaders in some less capable force.”

Cameraman Neil Davis (later killed in Thailand) had a chance to compare the Australians, and to look at their overall achievement.

Quoted in Tim Bowden, *One Crowded Hour*, Collins, Sydney, 1987, p. 143

> “I didn't go out with the Australians much, because relatively speaking they didn't do much fighting. They did have two or three very stiff battles, but that was over a period of several years. As an Australian I was very proud of the Australian troops. They were very professional, very well trained, and they fought the people they were sent to fight — the Viet Cong.
>
> They tried not to involve civilians and generally there were very few civilian casualties inflicted by the Australians.”

Journalist Hugh Lunn felt that the Vietnamese people liked the Australians because their uniform was different to the Americans, and they seemed to march everywhere. They also did not seem to threaten Vietnamese society. Lunn says that when Australia sent its national soccer team to a tournament in Saigon in 1967, many Viet Cong turned up to watch.[4] The Viet Cong, too, had a healthy respect for the Australian soldiers.

Hugh Lunn, *Vietnam: A Reporter's War*, UQP, Brisbane, 1986

> “[Dinh] said a Viet Cong colonel told him that he was very anti-Australian because he was born in Phuoc Tuy province where the Australians operated. The colonel told Dinh the Viet Cong feared the Australian night ambushes... The colonel was impressed that the Australian troops slept outside their camps and he said their preparation for a possible fight was very good.”

> “The modern Australian soldier in action also provides a contrast with the folk-images of the digger myth, so popularly accepted in the earlier wars which Australian citizen armies have fought. Like his Anzac forebear, the

Jane Ross in Peter King (ed), *Australia's Vietnam*, Allen & Unwin, Sydney, 1983

Australian soldier in Vietnam was credited with a fine performance, but in the new context of a regular professional army, whose effectiveness was seen as reflecting thorough training and firm discipline. ”

King (ed), *Australia's Vietnam*, p. 97

“ In contrast to American soldiers, the Australians in Vietnam seemed to constitute a homogeneous force, whose style was bland and inward-looking, whose behaviour and attitudes seldom betrayed any gross dissatisfaction with the army or the war. Their discontent was directed more towards their allies and towards those at home who did not provide the support or freedom of action which they would have liked. ”

What did they achieve?

The 4th Battalion was withdrawn from Nui Dat in November 1971, leaving the Army advisers as the only Australian soldiers still in Vietnam. Of the 50 000 Australians who had served in Vietnam by then, 496 had been killed, and 2398 wounded.

John Rowe, *Vietnam: The Australian Experience*, Time-Life, Sydney, 1987

“ They had fought courageously and brilliantly, had won every battle, and had cleared the enemy from vast areas of the land. But in the end, they, like the Americans, had accomplished little of lasting value, and the Asian jungles had closed over their efforts. ”

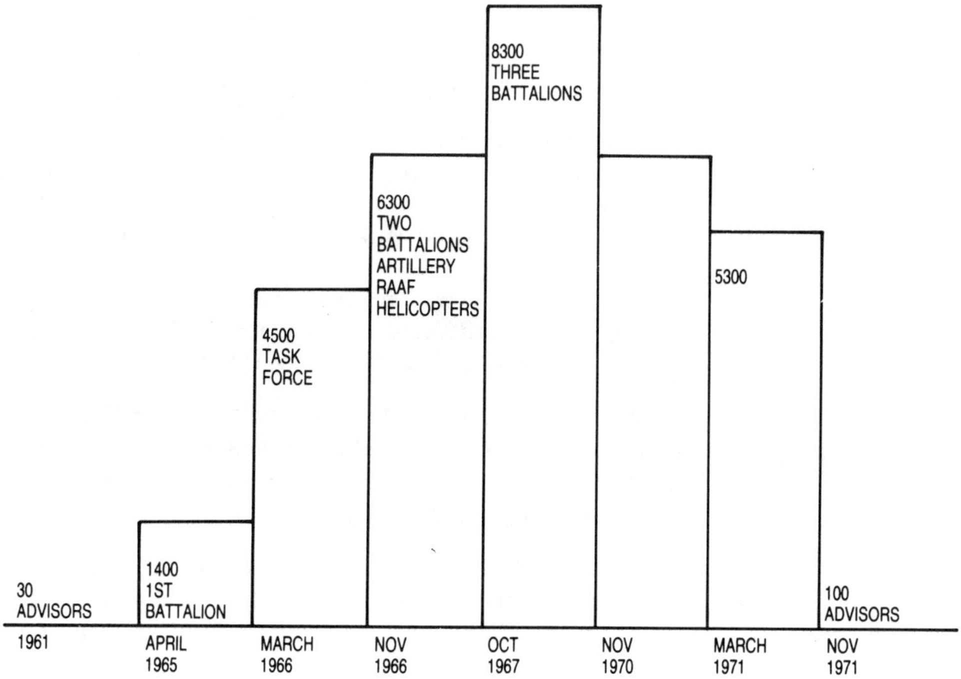

Australia's military commitment to Vietnam

Review

Outline the role of the Army, the Navy and the Air Force in Vietnam. How important was the contribution of each of these to the war?

Discuss

- What evidence is there that the Australians 'accomplished little of lasting value'?
- In what ways did the soldier in Vietnam differ from the Anzac digger?

Structured questions

- What was the aim of the Australian Government when it first committed Australian troops to Vietnam?
- How successful were the Australian troops in carrying out the various roles allocated to them?
- In what ways were the Australian aims, and the nature of the troops' involvement, likely to lead to dissatisfaction among the soldiers and opposition to the war back home?

DOCUMENT STUDY

Australian impact in Phuoc Tuy

The job of pacifying the province of Phuoc Tuy was given to the Australians. The Australians' base was set up at Nui Dat, and one of their first tasks was to clear the area within 4 km of the base. The town of Long Phuoc was destroyed in this process (Operation Enoggera) and its 3400 inhabitants were forced to move — their homes were destroyed, they were forbidden to engage in their means of livelihood, and they were given no help with resettlement, then or now. No compensation was paid for the land that was confiscated, and those Vietnamese who tried to obtain compensation were regarded as VC sympathisers and had their claims refused. One 60-year-old Vietnamese man expressed his attitude when interviewed in 1967:

> “Australians forbid people to go to work in the field. If who [sic] goes there secretly, he will be frightened by the helicopter then be captured and brought to the district town. Here we only live on agricultural produce, now we are forbidden to go working in the rice field. What do we live on?
>
> On these days we are allowed to go working in the fields twice a week, but we must come back by 4 pm. If he who comes back late will be blamed and his identity card seized and he will be on fatigue for two three days. This harvest is only obtained 3/10 [30 per cent].”

Quoted in Terry Burstall, *A Soldier Returns*, UQP, Brisbane, 1990, p. 178.

Terry Burstall, an Australian veteran of the Battle of Long Tan, has revisited Vietnam several times. These visits have caused him to question the role the Australians played in the conflict. During his research, he found this 1969 statement from the Task Force senior officers:

> “Display VC bodies (in some inoffensive manner) so that the villagers could see what the shooting was all about and what is being done for them by the Free World Forces. This may encourage them to increase their participation in their own defence.”

Burstall, *A Soldier Returns*, p. 71

Australian troops, shown during the destruction of the village of Long Phuoc (Australian War Memorial negative no. CUN/66/521/VN)

The community hall in the village of Long Phuoc, 1992. The village has been largely rebuilt since its destruction by Australian soldiers in 1966, but people in Long Phuoc remain justifiably wary of foreigners

In 1989 Burstall met and talked with Mrs Xiu, who lived near Nui Dat:

> "Mrs Xiu sat on one side of me and Thang on the other. On the table was an Australian hootchy, the small half-tent that infantrymen carry. I couldn't help myself. I touched the hootchy and felt one edge of it. Mrs Xiu spoke to me quickly and the sound of her voice startled me. I looked at Thang in confusion and his face was chalky as if he wanted to be sick. He translated softly that this was the thing 'your people' had sent my youngest son home in.
>
> I sat staring at the hootchy as if it were alive and the patches on it became bloodstains in my mind. Display VC bodies (in some inoffensive manner). I wonder if she thought it was inoffensive as she collected the mangled body of her son from the military post at Phuoc Loi...
>
> Mrs Xui must have been reading my mind or starting to feel the weight of her sorrow again because she said to me curtly, 'Why did you come here? What right did you have to destroy my sons? I had never heard of your country before your soldiers came here.'"

Burstall, *A Solider Returns*, pp. 83–5

Discuss

- An Army Civic Action unit was set up in June 1967 to improve relations with the Vietnamese. What problems would this unit have faced in its work?
- Who did the Army regard as the enemy?
- Why did the Army act in this manner in Vietnam?
- Terry Burstall feels that the reasons for the Army's attitude go back to Australia's original involvement. 'We were there because of the Americans and we gave little thought to the Vietnamese.'[5] Does this adequately explain its attitude?

WAR IN THE SOUTH

CHAPTER EIGHT

1965–1967

THE WAR in South Vietnam was seen by both sides as one of attrition — the gradual wearing down of the enemy's forces. General Westmoreland planned to stabilise key positions in Vietnam by setting up a series of firebases, and then sweep through large areas in Search and Destroy missions to clear the Viet Cong. He knew that this would take two years to show any real results, and the British advised him that it had taken twelve years for them to be successful in Malaya. The Viet Cong aimed to use a two-pronged strategy. Guerrilla forces would harass the enemy and keep control of the villages. Viet Cong regular forces, helped by soldiers from the Army of North Vietnam (NVA), would make occasional attacks against towns and installations. These attacks would also help to divert the enemy from anti-guerrilla activities, and would be made when and where it suited the Viet Cong, so that they always retained the initiative. The main difference in strategy was that the Americans were fighting for *positions*, the Viet Cong for control of the *people*, and they were starting with control of 90 per cent of the villages.

The attrition strategy could only work to the advantage of the Viet Cong, but the Americans failed to see this. Westmoreland's strategy of just another year or just another 100 000 soldiers became reminiscent of General Haig's performance in World War I. However, while Westmoreland might have been prepared to wait, the politicians in the USA were more impatient. President Johnson wanted quick results, preferably well before the November 1968 elections. The Viet Cong knew that the Americans would go home eventually, and they were prepared to fight for fifteen to twenty years. They also knew that a war of attrition would gradually become unpopular at home in America. Each Viet Cong soldier killed would only harden their resolve to win; each American soldier killed would only add to the unpopularity of the war at home and increase the pressure to get out.

> “The machinery which Ho and Giap had set up so effectively during the first war continued to function as effectively in the second, with a few adjustments to account for the greater American air power. For instance,

Giap learned how to counter American air power by joining battle so closely that American planes would kill Americans as well. But the style was the same — frustrate the enemy, wear them out, bog them down in the quagmire, make victory elusive, make for the Americans the only symbol of the war their own casualty lists. Like the French, the Americans could only control the land they stood on because, though they had total military superiority, the other side had total political superiority — it controlled the population. ”

Halberstam, *Ho*, p. 114

ROLE OF THE NORTH

The Americans claimed that the Viet Cong were controlled from the North, and that the US was fighting against the North to stop it from invading the South. The Viet Cong claimed to be independent of North Vietnam. The true relationship between the North and the Viet Cong was somewhere between these two extremes, but was difficult to define as it kept changing. By 1965, the National Liberation Front (NLF) had developed into a very strong political and military force that was largely independent. The North gave direction, and supplied about 20 per cent of the NLF's funds. Gradually, the direct military support increased. After the 1968 Tet Offensive, the NVA largely took over the fighting from the NLF forces.

	Estimated NVA Troops in South Vietnam	*US Troops in South Vietnam*	*Australian Soldiers*	*Others*
1964	2 500	16 000	100	
1965	11 000	200 000	1 400	
1966	50 000	300 000	4 500	
1968 (January)	60 000	520 000	8 300	4 500 (South Korea) 2 500 (Thailand) 300 (New Zealand)

The Chinese and the Soviets both provided supplies to North Vietnam, and these were passed onto the South along the Ho Chi Minh Trail. Mao Zedong recommended to the North Vietnamese that they wage a drawn-out war in the South, as he had done in China. Many North Vietnamese felt that Mao would like to see both Vietnam and the United States weakened by a long war.

The Viet Cong could survive on between 15 to 60 tonnes of supplies a day reaching them, but these generally had to be transported along the Ho Chi Minh Trail. In the early days, the journey could take up to six months.

“ Years later, the journey would take only six weeks, but with the same perils. In the long rainy season, September to February, catastrophic floods would constantly wash away the man-made trails, turning streams into rapids and the gorges into monstrous rivers. Flimsy, metre-wide bridges, with bamboo foot planks and ropes for handrails, were strung between the high peaks, then hastily dismantled to avoid detection. In the dense forests the knapsacks of the marchers were so weighted by the rains that the men could not walk upright. Then under the palest sun they would steam and suffocate. Malaria and amoebic dysentery were the main scourges. In the early days it was believed that ten per cent of those who set out died from disease. ”

Michael Maclear, *Vietnam: The Ten Thousand Day War*, Methuen, London, 1982, p. 239

Communist Organisation

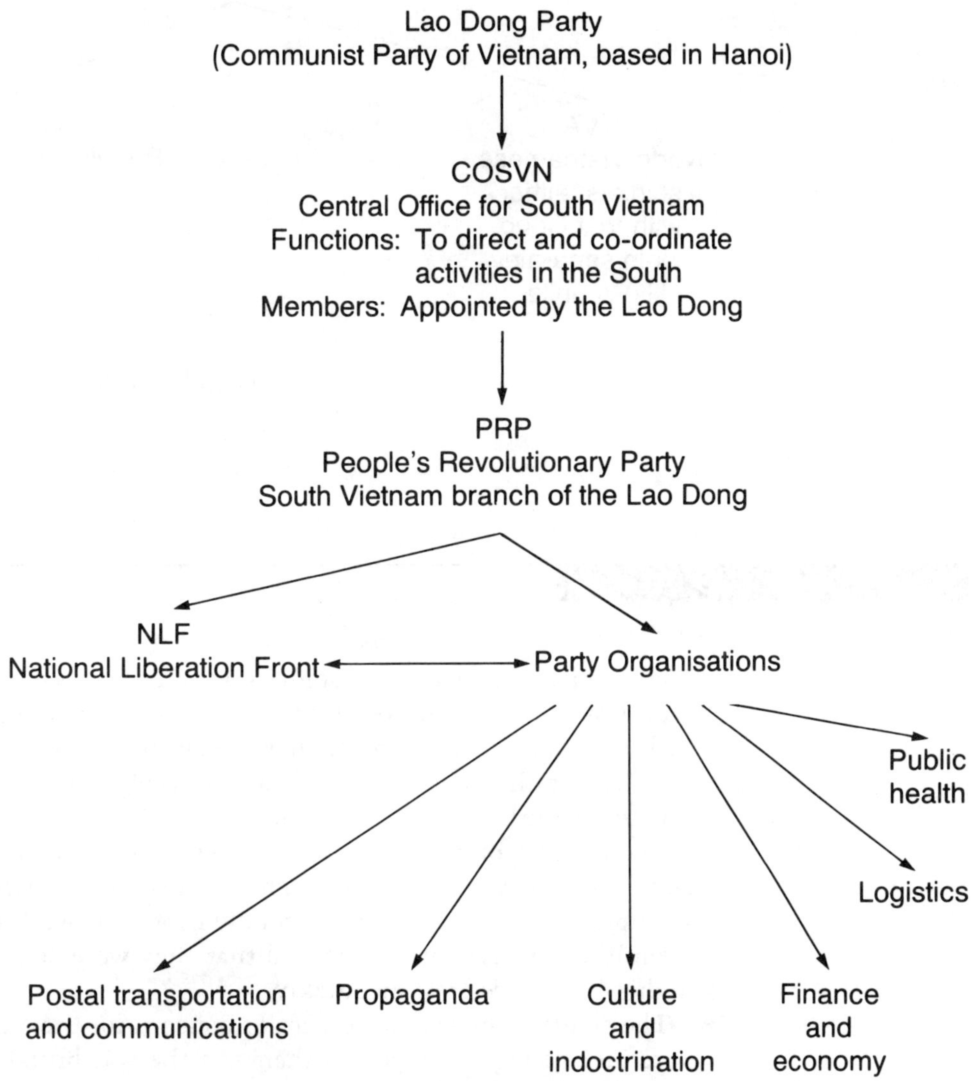

Adapted from information in Lex McAulay, *The Battle of Long Tan*, Arrow, London, 1987

Discuss

The Americans claimed that the NLF was controlled by the North Vietnamese, who denied this and claimed that the NLF was independent. Who was correct?

Communist Army Structure

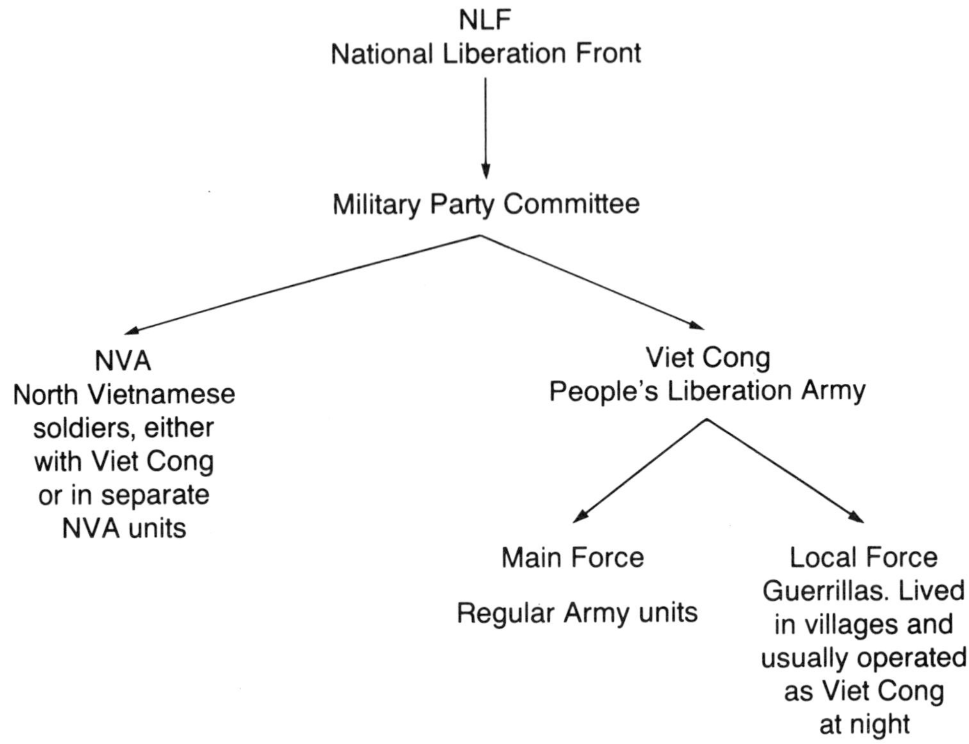

THE SOLDIERS

The average age of the US soldiers in Vietnam was 19, compared to 26 in World War II. The drafted (conscripted) soldiers went when they were 18, with some of them having their birthday on the way. They were kids with very little military training and no knowledge of the Vietnamese people or why they were being sent. Mark Baker's book *Nam* includes many of the soldiers' accounts. One of them was playing with his yo-yo one day and could not understand why his officer became so upset. Another had only been there a couple of days when he very proudly captured two Vietnamese and dragged them back to base, only to be told that they were South Vietnamese (ARVN) soldiers. The kids grew up quickly.

The soldiers showed no respect or concern for the Vietnamese people, who were just 'gooks' or 'slopes' to them. As the war brutalised the soldiers, they took their brutality out on the people:

> "Our base was pretty quiet. Sometimes you'd be going up to guard mount and the commander would tell us, 'Look, we haven't had many kills in a long time. So let's go down to the village and shoot somebody and drag them back across the river.' You weren't supposed to shoot them unless they were on our side of the river. He didn't say it in those words exactly, he just said, 'Hey, you know, you guys want a day off, we got to be getting more kills.' He'd kind of hint."

Mark Baker, *Nam*, Abacus, London, 1988, p. 134

> You don't want a prostitute. You've got an M-16. What do you need to pay for a lady for? You go down to the village and you take what you want... These were not men who would normally commit rape. They had not had psychological problems. Being in that kind of environment, you give a guy a gun and strange things happen.

Baker, *Nam*, p. 146

The soldiers usually had little respect for their officers, and in many cases this was well deserved. Most officers were only sent to Vietnam for six months, which was often a cause of resentment for the soldier serving out his twelve-month tour of duty. The standard of officer fell alarmingly during the war, as men with minimal training and limited intelligence were sent over. One officer who could not read a map led his men into a minefield. From 1968, the situation deteriorated and over 700 attacks on officers were reported. 'Fragging', the murder of officers, began, with eighty-three deaths officially recorded.

Poor leadership started at the top and worked its way down. The generals had trouble measuring success in a guerrilla war, so turned to statistics to help them. They started to talk of kill ratios and body counts, and there was pressure down the line to come up with a good body count.

> A twenty-four-year-old Special Forces captain was telling me about it. 'I went out and killed one VC and liberated a prisoner. Next day the major called me in and told me that I'd killed fourteen VC and liberated six prisoners. You want to see the medal?'

Michael Herr, *Dispatches*, Picador, London, 1979, p. 141

The generals took the statistics seriously and released them to the media who kept reporting back to America that the war was being won because the kill ratios were favourable.

The statistic that the US had 500 000 soldiers in South Vietnam hid the real weakness of their military effort. The appetite of the US Army for supplies was huge. It had to be supplied with the biggest and the best equipment, and the soldiers had to be given everything that they might get back home. Soldiers in battle had to be supplied with beer and ice-cream, and at night could watch on television what the weather had been like that day in California. The US 1st Cavalry Division needed 500 tonnes of supplies a day, which required a huge logistics effort. Almost 80 per cent of the soldiers in South Vietnam were in non-combat jobs — storemen, cooks, drivers, repairs. This left 100 000 to carry on the fighting, but at any one time up to half of these would be inactive. The Australian Army had up to 75 per cent of soldiers in combat positions.

US STRATEGY

Search and Destroy

Search and Destroy sweeps through areas were bound to fail. The Viet Cong melted into the jungle and re-emerged when the Americans left. The Americans were not trusted by the local peasants, and were given no intelligence as to the Viet Cong positions. This caused the Americans to overreact whenever they found any suspected area, and they would blanket it with artillery, bombing attacks, napalm and rockets. These attacks could destroy the whole area, but they could not separate the Viet Cong from the peasants and quite often it was the peasants who were affected. Robert Asprey refers to one Search and Destroy mission which in two weeks destroyed 65 per cent of the homes of the 17 000 people in the area.[1] The great majority of the peasants in South Vietnam had been untouched by the war up to 1965. The US escalation of the war quickly created half a million refugees who mostly moved to Saigon, adding greatly to the problems that the city already had.

Rolling Thunder

Operation Rolling Thunder had two aims: to attack the North and to cut off supplies along the Ho Chi Minh Trail. Despite the huge number of bombs dropped on the North, their morale was stronger than ever. The Americans found that a basically peasant society could carry on, and they were forced to start bombing the outskirts of Hanoi and Haiphong. This drew severe criticism of the United States from many countries. The bombing was also very expensive, as the Soviet Union had supplied the North with surface-to-air missiles. By the end of 1966, the US had lost 318 planes over the North.

Attacks on the Ho Chi Minh Trail had no more success. The B-52 bomber could drop a hundred 350-kilogram bombs in 30 seconds and clear a path through the jungle 1.5 kilometres long, but as Maclear points out, the effort was not worth the result. The bombing raids were only stopping one in every hundred North Vietnamese at a cost of 100 tonnes of bombs or $140 000.

DOCUMENT STUDY

“*Senator Thurmond*: Is there any reason why, if we want to win over North Vietnam, we can't put them on notice that we are going to bomb them and bomb them if necessary to bring this war to a close? That is what we did in Germany, wasn't it?

Admiral Sharp: I think that would probably be one thing that would bring it to the end.

Senator Thurmond: That would bring it to an end, wouldn't it?

Admiral Sharp: Yes, sir: one of the things we have to do to bring this war to an end is to demonstrate to the VC and the North Vietnamese beyond a shadow of a doubt that we are going to keep it up.

Senator Thurmond: That we have the will to win; we have the power to win; and that we are going to put the pressure on them until we do win.

Admiral Sharp: That is correct.

Senator Thurmond: And not have any letup *and not have any restraint: merely because a few civilians near military targets clamor about bombing* [emphasis added].

We could put them on notice to move the civilians, couldn't we, out of any areas we were going to bomb, if necessary?
Admiral Sharp: We could.
Senator Thurmond: Although I don't think we did that in World War II.
Admiral Sharp: I don't think we did, either.
Senator Thurmond: We just said we were going to win and we took the steps to win. We can do it here if we have the will to do it.
But if we are going to listen to world opinion or Communist propaganda or State Department propaganda, then we won't win. ”

'Air War Against North Vietnam'. Hearings before Senate Sub-committee, 90th Congress, 1st session. Washington, DC, 1967, p. 9

- What attitudes do the two men share towards the war and the Vietnamese?
- What historical precedent are they using to justify the bombing? Are they correct to use this as a precedent?

Helicopters

Helicopters were most valuable to the Americans when they were used to support troops in battle, or to evacuate wounded soldiers. The Americans could justifiably boast that any wounded soldier would be in hospital within thirty minutes, and that only 18 per cent of wounded soldiers died. The film *Frontline* gives a very clear view of just how devastating the helicopter could be when

This central display in the Military Museum, Hanoi, shows the wreckage of a B-52 bomber, shot down over Hanoi on the first night of Nixon's Christmas bombing campaign, December 1972. A Soviet MIG fighter sits symbolically on top

it was used as a gunship, in a scene showing it destroying a village. However, there were limitations to the helicopter's usefulness. They were noisy and very visible to the Viet Cong, who quickly learnt American helicopter tactics. Often the Viet Cong could predict the landing zone and ambush the Americans when they landed. Over 1400 helicopters were shot down by the end of 1967, and by 1973 the total exceeded 4000.

Review

- What help did the NLF receive from North Vietnam, China and the Soviet Union?
- Why were American soldiers unsuited to the fighting in South Vietnam?
- What were the main problems with the United States Army?
- What were Search and Destroy missions and Operation Rolling Thunder? Why did they fail?
- Were the Americans winning the war by late 1967?

THE ARVN

There were 500 000 ARVN soldiers killed in the war between 1963 and 1973, compared to 46 000 Americans, and there were only a few weeks during the war when the American death rate was higher than that of the South Vietnamese. The ARVN soldiers met the Viet Cong more on their own ground — in the paddy fields and jungles without the aid of massive support. The film *Frontline* shows these soldiers in action, and Neil Davis tells in the film of his respect for the ARVN soldiers.

Few people, though, could have respected the ARVN officers or the Army itself. There were over 500 000 soldiers in the South Vietnamese Army by 1968, but the annual desertion rate exceeded 20 per cent. Army pay was very poor, at about a sixteenth the rate for US soldiers, and the ordinary soldier had no chance of adding to his finances through corruption. He could only take what he wanted from the villagers. The ARVN officers had plenty of chances for corruption and made use of them all. The most common form of corruption, and the most costly, was ghosting. 'Ghost soldiers [according to Gabriel Kolko] were dead men, deserters or soldiers who held civilian jobs and whose superiors pocketed their pay and allowance.'[2] Up to one-quarter of the ARVN may have been ghosts.

The Americans were upset at the lack of effort that the South Vietnamese seemed to be making to win the war. In the cities, they could see many South Vietnamese men of military age enjoying life. Michael Maclear points out that their tactics in the war became known as 'Search and Avoid'.[3] The South Vietnamese Army clearly had no motivation. The conflict became a war that the Americans wanted to win more than the South Vietnamese did.

What were they fighting for?

Air Marshal Ky and General Thieu, who shared power in South Vietnam from 1965, paid lip service to democracy to keep the Americans happy, but they had no intention of implementing it. They continued to be backed by the generals and were not interested in sharing power. The abuses of the Diem regime remained and corruption was a way of life. Land reform was forgotten; landlords were even known to go out with the Army to collect back rent.

> "The peasant's main concern was not democracy but survival with dignity... No one had shown them democracy. People who would have directly suffered terror of the Communist takeover constituted, for the most part, a rapacious ruling minority whose greed and intransigence were keeping the nation, such as it was, in its turbulent, impotent condition."

Asprey, *War in the Shadows*, p. 1361

An election was held in September 1967 for a new Assembly, but the result was carefully organised. Communists and militant Buddhists were barred from standing, and other well known opponents of the government were stopped. If these measures failed, then the ballot boxes were stuffed. Thieu and Ky won the election, but more and more the Viet Cong were beginning to seem the only viable opposition.

EFFECTS ON THE SOUTH

The physical effects of the US presence in the South were profound, with engineers working around the clock to build roads, bridges, airfields and six deep water harbours. However, the effects on the people and society were catastrophic. Vietnamese society crumbled under the impact of the affluent US presence on what had been a poor country. Refugees fled to Saigon, either attracted by the new money or forced out of their homes by US raids. Sleazy bars and nightclubs flourished as many women turned to prostitution. Large gangs of delinquents roamed the Saigon streets.

Anything could be obtained on the black market, with turnover reaching $10 billion a year. US military equipment, from flak jackets to mortars, could be obtained. The going price for an M-16 rifle was $80. At times, the US military had to rent back some of its stolen jeeps at $250 a month. Watches, diamonds, marijuana and heroin could also be bought freely. Much of the money that the Americans poured in ended up in the hands of some of the urban Vietnamese and by 1968 $18 billion had been transferred to foreign bank accounts by them. United States' aid intended for the peasants was taken over by ARVN officers who then sold it to the peasants.[4]

Less than 100 metres from the Vietnamese National Assembly in Saigon, black market stalls operated, selling anything from whisky to cosmetics to fine china. Much of the merchandise was stolen from American warehouses (Photo by K. Sawada, 30 January 1970, UPI)

EFFECTS ON THE NORTH

The physical damage caused by the Rolling Thunder raids on North Vietnam was enormous. Huge areas were bomb-cratered, 85 per cent of electricity production was cut, and 100 000 people were killed. Despite this, the people found that they were brought closer together in their efforts to resist foreign attack. Effective civil defence saved many lives. Trenches and shelters were built, and 3 million access holes were dug throughout Hanoi to give immediate protection. Many people were evacuated from Hanoi and Haiphong. The Soviet Union provided radar, anti-aircraft guns and surface-to-air missiles that caused heavy losses for the US Air Force by 1967. The Soviet Union and China also provided food and other supplies to make up for disrupted production.

The Canadian writer Michael Maclear travelled through North Vietnam in 1969:

> “The awesome bomb craters along the 'highway' interlocked almost end to end, negotiable only by jeep... The journey showed that five cities had been leveled... each formerly with populations between 10 000 and 30 000. The North's third largest city, Nam Dinh — population 90 000 — was largely destroyed but at least recognizable... Across the whole landscape, journeying

far from the highway, not a single habitable brick edifice could be seen: the schools, hospitals, and administrative buildings that had certainly once existed were now, like the factories, just so many heaps of rubble. ”

Maclear, *Vietnam*, p. 334

Maclear found that the morale of the North had only been strengthened by the tremendous efforts that they had put in. Almost every bridge in the North was destroyed at least once, but they were rebuilt in many ingenious forms. Some were rebuilt just below the surface of the water, others were pontoons that were floated together at night.

In some ways, the war effort helped the Communist Government increase its popular support. Almost all agriculture had been organised into socialist

The main thing North Vietnam had going for it was its population. The Hanoi regime was able to mobilise people rapidly to repair damage caused by bombing (Marc Riboud/Magnum, courtesy of John Hillelson Agency Limited)

Pentagon personnel came to realise the futility of bombing North Vietnam because of the North's ability to keep supplies moving south by the simplest of contrivances such as bicycles (Marc Riboud/Magnum, courtesy of John Hillelson Agency Limited)

co-operatives by 1965, and the Government gave increasing responsibility to the co-operatives during the war. People in the North gained more freedom and continued to elect their village chiefs, unlike in the South. Women were encouraged into the rural workforce, and their efforts helped to keep agricultural production stable. North Vietnam also depended on the villages for industrial production, as attempts to develop industries in the cities were suspended.

> “They were managed provincially and locally after 1965, they used mainly their own raw materials, and their output required little transport. Above all, they were difficult for the Americans to bomb. Often involving little more than a small forge or a few machine tools in a hut or cave, this largely artisanal system produced everything from agricultural tools to pottery and electric motors.”

Kolko, *Vietnam*, p. 266

TRAN VAN TRUONG

Haiphong 1967

"In the summer of 1967 I was fifteen years old. There had been a lot of bombing already, but by that time everyone was prepared for it. We had a bunker dug into the floor of the house underneath the heavy divan. It was an excavation about four feet deep in the dirt floor, with the opening next to the divan, which served as a roof. That was a common kind of arrangement. Some families even slept in their bunkers during the worst times. But we never did that, even though I lived in a dangerous area, less than a mile from the harbor.

All of the students had also gotten training in school about how to treat wounds. Every house had a supply of bandages, alcohol, and cotton for first aid.

There were a lot of casualties. Friends of mine were killed, especially by the *bi* bombs. That means 'gravel' bombs, the kind that shoot out thousands of bearings when they explode. During the bombings I began to hate the Americans, really hate them. But I hadn't started out hating them. My family was classified 'bourgeois'. My father had been a small-scale merchant who bought and sold all kinds of goods. After the Communists took over it was very hard for him to make a living. Since I came from an unacceptable family background, I knew they wouldn't let me go to the university. So what kind of future would I have?

No one in my family liked the government. Of course you couldn't say anything to anyone about that. But inside the family we could be a little freer. I knew my father hated them. None of us would have minded at all if the Saigon army had invaded the North and liberated us from them. If the Americans were helping Saigon, then we thought that maybe they really would come someday.

But when the Americans started attacking Haiphong, I began to hate them. Before my mother got hurt in the bombing, in the summer of 1967, I was part of a crowd that captured one American pilot who was shot down. I saw the whole thing from the beginning. I was watching the planes attack and I saw plumes of white smoke streaming out of one of them. Then the parachute came open and he began to come down, almost as if it were coming right at me."

David Chanoff & Doan Van Toai, *Portrait of the Enemy*, I.B. Tauris, London, 1986 (This very valuable book tells the other side of the story through interviews with North Vietnamese, former Viet Cong and southern Opposition leaders.)

Discuss

- Why did Tran Van Truong's family dislike the North Vietnamese Government?
- How effective were the United States bombing raids?

THE VIET CONG

The cadres or political organisers were crucial to the Viet Cong main forces. They maintained contact between the officers and the soldiers, and could overrule the officers on military decisions if the soldiers were likely to object. They kept up the morale of the soldiers and provided friendship and support to them. This was made easier because the officers, cadres and soldiers were almost all from peasant backgrounds, unlike the ARVN where officers and soldiers were mostly from the cities but from different social classes. The cadres also kept up the political motivation for the soldiers, and two nights a week were spent in political discussions.

The Viet Cong soldiers knew that they had the most to gain from victory, and believed that they were fighting for a better life for themselves or their families. They also knew that soldiers would be first in line in any land redistribution. For the North Vietnamese soldiers, their families would be looked after if they were killed and their children given preference for education and jobs.[5] The cadres helped, then, to develop a highly motivated force that relied on consensus and mutual support rather than on strict military discipline. It was not an army that was fighting for Communism. The Viet Cong was fighting to improve people's lives and for nationalism — to unify the country and rid it of foreign domination.

The Americans found it difficult to combat the effective use of the environment by the Viet Cong. Its headquarters were set up in an elaborate series of tunnels around Cu Chi, about 70 kilometres from Saigon. There were about 300 kilometres of tunnels in the network, and whole regiments could move through them and reappear, ready to fight. The Americans and Australians destroyed some sections, but not the main tunnels.

The Americans also tried to deny the Viet Cong the advantage that the jungle provided for guerrilla fighting. From 1962, the US carried out Operation Ranch Hand, which used chemicals to wipe out the jungle. The informal motto of the Ranch Hand pilots was 'Only we can stop the jungle'. The most infamous of the chemicals used was Agent Orange, which contained dioxin, a powerful carcinogen. Nineteen million gallons (about 86 million litres) of chemicals were used over the next ten years, and over a quarter of South Vietnam was affected. The main areas that were defoliated were suspected Viet Cong supply routes, along the river banks in the Mekong Delta, along the Demilitarised Zone, and around US and Australian bases and airfields. Defoliation did not stop Viet Cong movement. Its main result was a devastating and long-lasting effect on the environment and the people of South Vietnam.

Review

- What impact did the United States presence have on the society and economy of South Vietnam? What was the physical effect on North Vietnam?

- Complete the following table. You may either write in brief answers or rate each aspect as 'high', 'average' or 'low'.

Aspect	*NLF Army (Viet Cong)*	*ARVN*	*US Army*
Motivation			
Leadership			
Morale			
Weapons			
Tactics			
Relationship with peasants			
Support in cities			

Research

What weapons were used by the Viet Cong in the jungle?

Update

- What evidence remains in Vietnam today of the effect of the United States presence?
- What have been the effects of defoliation in Vietnam?
- How successful has (North) Vietnam been in rebuilding its cities and industries?
- What help has Vietnam received from the United States, the Soviet Union and China to rebuild since the war?

Structured questions

- (a) What was General Westmoreland's policy of attrition?
  (b) Why was it likely to fail?
- How effective was the ARVN in the war from 1965 to 1967?
- Why, despite the efforts of the ARVN and the US Army, were the NLF (Viet Cong) and the North Vietnamese not defeated?

DOCUMENT STUDY

Guerrilla life

Most of the Viet Cong spent many years living in guerrilla camps in South Vietnam. These camps were usually set up in jungle areas close to their supply lines from the Ho Chi Minh trail. The guerrillas were a mixture of cadres who had moved down from North Vietnam and South Vietnamese who had been recruited to fight against the Americans and their 'puppets'. They would usually live either in or close to tunnels where they could gain protection from bombs, often dropped from high altitudes by B-52s. Often they would get advance warning from Soviet trawlers in the South China Sea, or from observers in Thailand and would be able to hide in the underground tunnels.

on 21 January, General Westmoreland took this as the start of the offensive, whereas the North Vietnamese saw it as a ploy to distract attention from the cities where the Viet Cong would attack.

KHE SANH

Khe Sanh is a hilly area only 10 kilometres from Laos and 20 kilometres from the dividing line between North and South Vietnam. The Americans set up a base there in early 1967, probably to prepare for an expected attack on the Ho Chi Minh Trail through Laos. The physical setting was very much like Dien Bien Phu, and by late 1967 the NVA had dug their artillery into the hills around Khe Sanh to prepare for an attack. During January, they moved about 40 000 troops into the area to surround the 6000 US Marines and ARVN soldiers on Khe Sanh. On 21 January, a huge artillery barrage started the siege that was to last until the North Vietnamese were forced to withdraw in early April. Unlike Dien Bien Phu, the Americans had plenty of heavy artillery and a huge air superiority. Raids by B–52s and other bombers dropped 100 000 tonnes of bombs around Khe Sanh, and accounted for most of the estimated 10 000 NVA casualties. Conditions for the besieged troops were very difficult as they were forced to dig into the hilltop for protection from the almost constant shelling. All supplies, including water, had to be brought in by air, which was extremely hazardous. Five hundred Americans died in the siege. Many of them were killed in planes that were shot down as they tried to land or take off.

Both General Westmoreland and President Johnson made Khe Sanh a test of their credibility, and the battle took on an importance that it barely deserved.

A Marine lance corporal armed with an M–14 fires at an enemy forward observer outside the Khe Sanh perimeter (source unknown)

It also became important to the United States public who could watch the progress of the battle every night on television. Reporters who were sufficiently foolhardy could visit Khe Sanh, and their reports and film had great impact. If this was Westmoreland's attrition policy in action, then the American public did not like it.

For the North Vietnamese, it was the first major battle where the NLF (Viet Cong) played no part. Although their losses were high and they did not capture Khe Sanh, it must still be seen as a Communist victory:

- It drew American troops away from the cities in the South, and diverted attention from them for the Tet Offensive.
- It played a major part in the change in US public opinion.
- In June 1968, the Americans abandoned Khe Sanh and the North Vietnamese reclaimed it without a fight. If the Khe Sanh area was so important strategically, then it was under North Vietnamese control after this.

THE TET OFFENSIVE

Tet is the celebration of the lunar New Year, and had been a traditional ceasefire period in Vietnam. (It was also the anniversary of a famous Vietnamese victory over the Chinese in 1789, so it had not always been a time for ceasefire.) Ho Chi Minh was already ailing, and many people thought that this would be his last Tet. (He died in September 1969.) On the day before the Tet attacks began, a poem written especially by Ho Chi Minh for the occasion was read over Radio Hanoi.

> “This spring far outshines the previous springs,
> Of victories throughout the land come happy tidings.
> Let North and South emulate each other in fighting the United States aggressors!
> Forward! Total victory will be ours!”

The next day, 30 January, seven major cities were attacked and on 31 January one hundred separate attacks were made across all of South Vietnam, including attacks on thirty provincial capitals. The Americans were stunned that the Communist forces, mostly NLF (Viet Cong), could attack so many places at the one time. Their vast intelligence network had failed to warn them of the attacks, just as it had failed to provide a warning about Pearl Harbour in 1941. Prime Minister Thieu had given most of the ARVN soldiers a holiday, and was taking one himself.

About 4000 Viet Cong were smuggled into Saigon in late January, with weapons and ammunition, and in the early hours of 31 January they attacked key targets. A select group blasted their way into the American embassy compound. Fighting went on for six hours before all nineteen commandos were killed. The US public could watch the fighting inside the walls of their own embassy that night on television, and see their ambassador interviewed

the bodies in the United States Embassy in Saigon, the shooting of a helpless captive by a police chief, the fighting at Khe Sanh and Hué.'[1] More importantly, influential media commentators changed their approach. The respected Walter Cronkite asked on television, 'What the hell is going on? I thought we were winning the war?'. Vocal elements of the population — media commentators, business executives, teachers, clergy and others — were now openly criticising Johnson. These groups were now of the opinion that the war was not worth the internal divisions and the threats to US power around the world.

JOHNSON'S DECISION

This change came at a crucial time for President Johnson, as it destroyed what was left of his credibility. Already, his social and economic policies were unpopular, and his overall approval rating had dropped to 36 per cent. Only 26 per cent of the people approved of his conduct of the war. Problems were also building up in other parts of the world. Tension was high in Korea after the seizure by the North Koreans in January of the US ship *Pueblo* and its crew of ninety-three. March also saw a crisis for the US dollar, a rush to sell it that threatened the United States' position in the world economy. To add to Johnson's problems, General Westmoreland requested 206 000 more troops for South Vietnam. Something had to give. According to Stanley Karnow: 'After Tet the administration finally acknowledged that any increase of troops to Vietnam threatened not just the country's economy but all of its domestic and international priorities'.[2]

Johnson tried to settle the troop request by handing it over to a committee headed by his new Secretary of Defense, Clark Clifford. The retiring Secretary of Defense, Robert McNamara, had been one of the strongest supporters of the war, but by late 1967 he had changed from a hawk to a dove so Johnson dumped him. Clifford started as a hawk, but after gathering evidence for the committee, he also changed his views. Clifford decided that there was no guarantee a further 200 000 troops would assure success, and that the United States should stop escalating the war and start handing over to the South Vietnamese. As Johnson was not likely to accept his views, Clifford brought together a group of leading Americans, the 'Wise Men', to try to influence the President. By late March, Westmoreland's request for 206 000 troops was denied.

President Johnson was also under enormous political pressure as the race for the presidential election in November 1968 was now underway. Senator Eugene McCarthy, the only clear anti-war candidate, nearly defeated Johnson in the New Hampshire primary election in February. Bobby Kennedy announced in mid-March that he would also challenge Johnson for the Democratic Party nomination, and made it clear that Vietnam would be an issue. Johnson's health started to crack under the strain, and he appeared to be losing his grip. On 31 March he made a televised speech to announce the end of the air and naval bombardment of North Vietnam, and to express the hope that this would lead to negotiations. He concluded by announcing his withdrawal from the presidential race:

> "I have concluded that I should not permit the presidency to become involved in the partisan divisions that are developing in this political year. Accordingly, I shall not seek, and I will not accept, the nomination of my party for another term as your President."

EFFECTS ON THE ARMIES

The United States Army started to disintegrate as an effective fighting force after the Tet Offensive. Most of the soldiers were aware that the war was winding down. Their President had given up hope of a military victory, and was looking for a political way out. The soldiers' main aim became survival for their twelve months tour of duty, and their motto was, 'Don't be the last GI to die in Nam'. Officers who ordered the grunts to undertake unnecessary or hazardous attacks were often fragged. Patrols tried to avoid contact with the Viet Cong. Army strategy changed and Search and Destroy missions were dropped. The Army turned much more towards guerrilla warfare, but lacked the experience of the Viet Cong. Living conditions for the 10 per cent of soldiers who were actually fighting became barely tolerable. Soldiers turned to drugs, with an estimated 56 per cent using marijuana and 22 per cent, heroin. By 1971, four times as many soldiers were in hospital for drug abuse than for combat wounds.[3]

The South Vietnamese Army was already an ineffective fighting force, with no prospect of improvement. American policy put greater pressure on it, with the policy of Vietnamisation adopted from 1968: to build up the size of the ARVN and hand over the fighting to them. Adding 200 000 soldiers only made South Vietnam's economic problems worse, and meant that there were 200 000 more soldiers to loot the villagers. No one seriously believed that the ARVN could succeed.

The Viet Cong had been greatly weakened by Tet, and needed time to rebuild. The North Vietnamese Army increasingly took over its role in the war. This process weakened the influence of the South Vietnamese Communists, and gave the North Vietnamese a stronger presence in the South. The war became less a civil war in the South, and more a takeover by the North. This has been the pattern up to the present, and southern resentment of northern influence is an important factor in today's Vietnam.

"*From* The Evening Star *(Washington):*
As the situation grows worse in Binh Dinh, air strikes are flown over populated areas.

A U.S. pilot back from a raid said: 'I killed 40 Viet Cong today. That's the number they told me were in the village, anyway, and I leveled it.'"

"*From the Cleveland* Plain Dealer *(excerpted from Sgt. Dennis Pena's letter to his parents):*
What I didn't like was when we burned the village down. The women and kids were crying and begging you not to burn them down. A lot of them stay inside and you have to drag them out.

Ma, that's not good to see. I look back at what was once a village and the people crying, but as the sergeant told me, that's war. I guess he was right."

In the Name of America, Turnpike Press, Virginia, 1968, pp. 105–6, 140

Read the above documents carefully. Below are three possible theories for the My Lai massacre. Do these documents confirm any of these theories?

- It was an isolated incident, not typical of the US Army.
- It was an inevitable consequence of the involvement of the US Army in Vietnam.
- It was typical of the methods and attitudes that developed in the US Army.

Review

- What was the significance of Khe Sanh for (a) the Americans and (b) the Communists?
- Why did the Communists launch the Tet Offensive? Outline the main events in the offensive.
- In what ways was Tet a military victory but a psychological defeat for the Americans?
- Why did Lyndon Johnson withdraw as a presidential candidate?
- What effects did Tet have on the US Army?
- What were the consequences of the Tet Offensive for the NLF/Viet Cong and for the North Vietnamese Army? How did the war change the relationship between the two?

Discuss

- *We had to destroy the town to save it.* What does this reveal of American attitudes and policy?
- *I sent the Army a good boy and they made him a murderer.* This comment was made by the mother of one of the men in Lieutenant Calley's platoon. Is this an apt verdict on the events of My Lai?

Structured questions

- Describe what happened in the Tet Offensive.
- Could the Tet Offensive have been seen as a success for the Communists?
- In what ways did the Tet Offensive mark a turning point in the war in Indo China?

THE HOME FRONT

CHAPTER TEN

AUSTRALIA

AUSTRALIA'S INVOLVEMENT in Vietnam did not concern or interest most Australians at the time. Coupled with a traditional apathy to politics was a 'Government knows best' attitude. Interest in the war was only intense among people who were directly affected by it, or in more politically active areas such as universities, trade unions and some churches. In universities, Vietnam became the protest issue that students had been looking for: proof that the older generation could not run the world. They agreed with Abbie Hoffman that no one over 30 could be trusted. The comfortable affluence of the 1960s meant that students could direct their energies into protests without worrying too much about getting a well paid job. The 1960s also saw many trade unions start to take an interest in political issues. The Waterside Workers Federation was particularly active, and banned the loading of supplies to Vietnam on a number of occasions.

Some church leaders were amongst the first to oppose the war openly. In March 1965, a month before Menzies announced that Australian troops would be sent, nine Anglican bishops sent a letter to him asking for the Government to look for a peaceful solution. In May 1965, 100 Methodist clergy staged a vigil for peace outside Parliament House. However, opposition to the war tended to come from individual clergy rather than from the church organisations. The Catholic Church was opposed to the anti-war protests, but many individual priests felt it was their duty to oppose an immoral war. In 1970 the Reverend Trathen, headmaster of Newington College (Sydney), advised 20-year-olds to defy the National Service Act. The College Council forced him to resign.

The first anti-war banners appeared at the Hiroshima Day marches on 9 August 1964, but no serious protests developed until after the introduction of conscription (November 1964) and the decision to send Australian troops (March 1965). Numerous protest groups sprang up, but they were more

"Police had followed a car in which Matteson was returning from a press interview, stopped it, and jumped into the backseat, handcuffing themselves to him. The astute driver immediately headed into the University grounds and sounded the alarm. With the help of boltcutters, students separated Matteson from his captors and guided him to safety."

King, *Australia's Vietnam*, p. 125

Review

- Amongst which sections of the Australian community did opposition to the war develop? Why?
- Why did some protest groups become more radical from 1967 onwards?
- What was the difference between the protest movement and the resistance movement?

THE MORATORIUM MOVEMENT

On 15 October 1969 the first Moratorium Day was held in the United States. Hundreds of thousands of people stopped work to join in the mass protest calling for the end of the war. The idea was picked up in Australia and a meeting was held in Canberra in November to co-ordinate an Australian campaign. Three separate campaigns were eventually held in May and September 1970 and June 1971.

Thousands turned out for this Vietnam moratorium march on 8 May 1970, one of the more peaceful demonstrations with few clashes between protestors and police (Mirror Australian Telegraph Publications)

DOCUMENT STUDY

MORATORIUM BROADSHEET

300,000 LEAFLETS

300,000 Moratorium leaflets, many with colour photographs, have been printed for distribution to every household in Adelaide, suburbs, and major country towns. This activity is essential to the success of the Moratorium. It is the only way in which the blatant misinformation spread by the mass media can be counteracted. YOUR HELP IS VITAL.

MASS MARCH & RALLY, SATURDAY MAY 9 AT 10 a.m.

Assemble Elder Park Rotunda at 10 a.m. Up King William St. to Victoria Sq., where music, speeches and street theatre will be staged. Speakers will include Hon. D.A. Dunstan, Q.C., M.P. (Leader of the S.A. Opposition), the prominent unionist Mr. Jim Shannon, Secretary of the S.A. Trades & Labor Council, and Mrs. Freda Brown, Federal President of the Union of Australian Women, recently returned from North Vietnam. Other speakers will include representatives of the student body and businessmen. Similar demonstrations will occur in all other States. They are one of the few legal but relatively inexpensive means of expressing our views publicly. If a demonstration is sufficiently large and spectacular it receives free TV and press coverage. ALTHOUGH YOU DISAPPROVE OF THE WAR IN VIETNAM, UNLESS YOU SHOW SOME CLEAR SIGN OF OPPOSITION, YOUR SILENCE WILL BE INTERPRETED AS CONSENT. THUS, BY FAILING TO ACTIVELY OPPOSE THE WAR YOU WILL HELP TO SUPPORT IT. MAKE THIS THE LARGEST DEMONSTRATION ADELAIDE HAS EVER SEEN.

Against The War . . .

Clearly the Vietnam war is not ending. The policies of 'Vietnamization' and 'progressive withdrawal' are in fact an attempt to end opposition to the war, rather than to end the war itself, to placate outraged public opinion while the war goes on. Responding to this situation Australians from all walks of life will organise and participate in a series of protests against the war culminating in nationally co-ordinated action during the week ending May 8-9-10. This is the Vietnam Moratorium Campaign a Moratorium against business as usual to end the war now.

Its objectives are:

IMMEDIATE withdrawal of Australian and all other foreign troops from Vietnam;

IMMEDIATE repeal of the National Service Act.

All Moratorium activities in pursuance of these objectives shall be of a non-violent nature. The campaign in N.S.W. is directed by a body of sponsors which is open to all who support these objectives. It aims to provide all Australians opposed to the war with an opportunity to publicly declare their commitment to strike against the war.

VIETNAM MORATORIUM CAMPAIGN MAY 8.9.10

OTHER ACTIVITIES:—

Thursday	**April 23. Poetry Reading and music** 8 p.m. Aldgate Crafts. Admission $1. Wine & cheese provided.
Friday	**April 24. Dr. Jim Cairns** Speaking at CPV Moratorium Mobilisation Meeting. 8 p.m. Union Hall, University of Adelaide.
Saturday	**April 25. MOTORCADE, ANZAC DAY** Meet at Wellington Hotel, Nth. Adelaide, 12 noon.
Sunday	**April 26. JAZZ** Jazz, blues and folk concert. 8 p.m. Union Hall, University of Adelaide. Admission 70c.
Tuesday	**April 28. POETRY & FOLK-SINGING** City Cross Arcade, 12–2 p.m.
Friday **Saturday**	**May 1] MOTORCADE to** **May 2] Whyalla & Port Augusta** Leaving Adelaide 2.30 p.m., Friday. Phone George Hutchesson, 38 1150 for more details.
Saturday	**May 2. Concert by Richard Meale** 19th Century & modern music. Matthew Flinders Theatre, Flinders University. 8 p.m. Admission $2.
Monday	**May 4. 'SOME WON'T GO'** American anti-conscription film; discussion with guest speakers. 7.45 p.m. Willard Hall, Wakefield St.
Monday-Friday	**Occupation of a Public Place May 4–8** Volunteers needed for 2 hr. shifts. Total environment provided by panel of artists. Details from VMC, 305 North Tce. Phone 23 2755.
Friday	**May 8. 24 hr. Strike** S.A. branch of Seaman's Union in support of Moratorium, starting 12 midnight, Thursday.

enquiries to: v.m.c.
305 north terrace, adelaide 5000

Photograph by John A. Ogle

- What evidence is there from the given sources that the moratorium movement was aimed at attracting much wider support than the traditional protest group base within Australia? Was it successful in this?
- What types of activities were there in the moratoriums? How did these differ from previous protest groups?
- What did the moratoriums hope to achieve?

Effects of the moratoriums

Focus questions

Read the accounts below of some of the people involved with or affected by the moratorium movement. Talk to people about the period.

- Did the protest movements have any effect on government policy?
- What effects did they have on the people involved?
- What do you think your attitude might have been to the moratorium movement?

“Looking back, the Vietnam demos don't seem to have been much *fun*. Perhaps too many of us had feelings similar to mine. There were all sorts of people on the marches, but a great many of us were university students like myself, many of us too young to have discovered our own direction in life, yet acting as if we had all the answers. The marches were rather dour affairs, with only slight touches of colour. The songs were heartrending, the atmosphere rebellious, and there was an air of hostility between ourselves and those who disagreed with us — our government, our police force, our returned soldiers, large sections of our community, even our own uncommitted friends. I am sure that many of us did march out of a belief in a new and better order, but for myself, and I imagine for many others too, I was motivated by a sense of horror at the war, and did not have much vision of the future. That is why, in my description of the marches, I have avoided the terms 'peace march' and 'peace movement', and have talked instead of the anti-war movement. For me at least, one thing which the Vietnam marches signally lacked was any sense of peace. ”

Charlotte Clutterbuck in Maddock & Wright (eds) *War: Australia and Vietnam*, p. 145

“ I suppose I had this idea of coming home to a brass band and ticker-tape processions and women falling at your feet and guys coming up and shaking your hand and all that sort of stuff — the way it was for the Anzacs and the Second World War guys.

I think we landed at Sydney airport about ten or eleven o'clock at night, went through customs, and got our pay. When the doors opened up there were these people waving placards and someone was holding up a page out of a newspaper about women and children being killed. ”

Bob Pride in Stuart Rintoul, *Ashes of Vietnam*, Heinemann, Melbourne, 1987, p. 182

“ I copped some flak in my home town. A woman who taught me at school spat at me. She was in the Save Our Sons. Yeah, spat at me and I adored that woman. The best teacher I'd ever had I thought. You remember one or two teachers in your life and she was a magnificent woman. I didn't think any less of her; she had her axe to grind. It was just surprising more than anything else. ”

Bob Walker in Rintoul, *Ashes of Vietnam*, p. 189

'YOU DON'T KNOW' SHOUTS DIGGER

BRISBANE, Fri.: A wounded Vietnam veteran stood on a crutch at the moratorium rally in Roma street yesterday and told 5000 protesters: "You wouldn't know what it's — well all about."

The crowd heard him almost in complete silence. There was a cheer or two.

Donald William Tate (21), who was wounded in the right leg and thigh in Vietnam last year, tried to grab the microphone from Labor Senator organisers.

Sen. Keeffe bent and asked what he wanted and then introduced him to the crowd as a wounded Digger.

Tate told the crowd: "I've been there and you haven't.

"What would one per cent of you know about how it really is over there.

"The allies are right to fight and Nixon is right to be in Cambodia.

"North Vietnam is the aggressor."

Tate then shouted that the rally was Communist-inspired and organised and was eventually jeered from the platform.

Border Morning Mail, 9 May, 1970

“ It cannot be shown that the anti-war movement influenced the federal government to withdraw Australian troops from Vietnam more quickly than it would otherwise have done. However, the government was clearly anxious about the degree of opposition to the war and to conscription within Australia. Its concern that Australian forces in Vietnam be withheld from the thick of the fighting, and its own furious attacks on the peace movement during the moratorium years indicate that the movement was seen to be a threat to its political and electoral fortunes. Certainly the movement influenced the ALP; the speed and obvious enthusiasm with which the Whitlam government removed the last traces of Australian military involvement in Vietnam and of conscription testify to this. ”

Malcolm Saunders, *The Anti-Vietnam War Movement in Australia: 1962–1973*, Canberra, 1982

THE UNITED STATES

The youth of America became more politically aware during the Kennedy years (1961–1963) when it seemed that one of their generation was in power and that the world could be changed. Their idealism was activated and they went off to join the Peace Corps or the civil rights movement. Bob Dylan's 'The Times They Are A'Changin' became their anthem. This idealism soured after the death of Kennedy and with the Vietnam War a lot of bitterness was turned on their government and society.

> “ The war seemed to sum up the evils of our society: destruction of people, destruction of environment, depersonalized use of technology, war by the rich and powerful against the poor and helpless... hypocrisy and lies, and a demand that the individual, regardless of his conscience, values or self, make himself into a part of the war machine. ”

Charles Reich, quoted in Hugh Higgins, *Vietnam*, Heinemann, London, 1975, p. 96

> “ To see ourselves newly and suddenly as the 'bad guys' in the world's polarity and to know the agent was 'my own government' was a development with serious consequences. Distrust for and even disgust with government were the most serious, beginning with alienation from the vote. 'You voted in '64 and got Johnson — why bother?' read a banner at an anti-war rally in New York. ”

Barbara Tuchman, *The March of Folly*, Michael Joseph, London, 1984, p. 340

> “ The longer the Vietnam War lasted the more people began to appreciate just how powerful (the military-industrial complex) had become and to realize the consequences of having so much power concentrated in such hands. The war did not create the military-industrial complex; it did, however, emphasize its influence. ”

Higgins, *Vietnam*, p. 98

Discuss

- What is meant by the military-industrial complex?
- What influence could it have? Why would some people oppose it?

The draft system worsened the divisions in American society, with college students being able to have their draft deferred. This favoured the middle class and meant that a disproportionate number of blacks and poorer whites were drafted. Once in the Army, blacks had a greater chance of becoming

A Vietnam veteran hurls back his war decoration at an anti-Vietnam rally in Washington, DC in 1971. What was the significance of this action? (Bernard Martell)

combat troops. Recent US Vice President, Dan Quayle, was one person who avoided the draft and a study estimated there were 15 million others.[7] Vietnam was also an important issue in the 1992 election, in which President Clinton was called unpatriotic for his opposition to the war.

Opposition to the war was strong from the start, with one gathering of 25 000 protesting in March 1965 against the sending of combat troops. Up to 1968, the strength of the movement was on the campuses, and protests took varied forms. Sit-ins and teach-ins were held, draft cards burnt, and attempts made to stop troop trains. In 1967 the group, Vietnam Veterans Against the War, was formed. In October 1967, tens of thousands of demonstrators staged a march on the Pentagon in Washington DC, but were held back by 10 000 troops. However, it was at the Democratic Party Convention in Chicago in August 1968 that the different parts of the anti-war movement came together, as opponents of the war gathered to see if the Democrats would choose the anti-war Eugene McCarthy or Johnson's Vice President, Hubert Humphrey, as their candidate.

Amongst those who came to Chicago were:

- The National Mobilization Committee, led by Dave Dellinger, a radical Quaker pacifist and organiser of the Pentagon March. His assistant was Tom Hayden, former leader of Students for a Democratic Society, and they hoped to attract up to 100 000 peaceful protesters to Chicago.
- McCarthy supporters. Eugene McCarthy was very popular amongst the

young, but had not gained substantial support from within the Democratic Party.

- The Yippies, or Youth International Party. Led by Jerry Rubin and Abbie Hoffman, they were political hippies, with some strange ideas, as outlined in one of their pamphlets.

YIPPIE!
Lincoln Park
VOTE PIG IN 68
Free Motel
'come sleep with us'
REVOLUTION TOWARDS A FREE SOCIETY: YIPPIE!
By A. Yippie

1. An immediate end to the War in Vietnam...
2. Immediate freedom for Huey Newton of the Black Panthers and all other black people. Adoption of the community control concept in our ghetto areas...
3. The legalization of marihuana and all other psychedelic drugs...
4. A prison system based on the concept of rehabilitation rather than punishment.
5. ... abolition of all laws related to crimes without victims. That is, retention only of laws relating to crimes in which there is an unwilling injured party, i.e. murder, rape, assault.
6. The total disarmament of all the people beginning with the police. This includes not only guns, but such brutal devices as tear gas, MACE, electric prods, blackjacks, billy clubs, and the like.
7. The Abolition of Money. The abolition of pay housing, pay media, pay transportation, pay food, pay education, pay clothing, pay medical help, and pay toilets.

Quoted in Norman Mailer, *Miami and the Siege of Chicago*, Penguin, Harmondsworth, 1969, p. 133

Supporters of these three groups were met by Chicago's formidable Mayor Richard Daley and his police force. Daley told Walter Cronkite on television that police brutality was the only alternative to allowing 'a lawless violent group of terrorists to menace the lives of millions of our people'.[8] His police obliged during the convention, with their brutality reaching its height on the last night (28 August) when they went berserk.

> "At 7:50 p.m. the crowd was mounting outside the hotel. It was clear, however, that the demonstrators would not be allowed to march on the convention. Only the Poor People's mule train was allowed through the police lines to proceed up Michigan Avenue. There was a lot of confusion as nobody seemed to know what to do. Most of the demonstrators were obviously still suffering from the tear-gas attack that had broken up the attempt to form a march an hour earlier. There was no effective leadership, though there was a ragged attempt to stage a sit-down demonstration. I'd say most of them were pacifically inclined middle-class kids. There were some hippies, but probably just as many Chicago citizens rubbernecking. Then at 8 p.m. it happened. Cohorts of police began to charge into the crowd from a street north of the Hilton, Balbo. The kids screamed and were beaten to the ground by cops who had completely lost their cool. Some tried to surrender by putting their hands on their heads. As they were marched to vans to be arrested, they were rapped in the genitals by the cops' swinging billies. I saw one girl, surrounded by cops, screaming, 'Please God, help me. Help

me.' A young man who tried to help got his head bloodied by a flailing club. Some of the demonstrators were thrown against a window of the hotel and pushed through it. The cops were using Mace indiscriminately. But then there was no discrimination about any of it. One policeman I overheard said with a delighted smile, 'They're really getting scared now.' It was a sadistic romp. One of the more unforgettable vignettes was of an Illinois politician, he must have been a state senator, sauntering out of the front door of the hotel to observe the carnage. A police sergeant turned from the beating that was going on at his feet and inquired politely, 'How are you this evening, Senator?' 'Fine,' said the senator, puffing on his cigar, 'just fine.' ”

Lewis Chester, G. Hodgson & B. Page, *An American Melodrama: The Presidential Campaign of 1968*, Andre Deutsch, London, 1969, p. 5

The opponents of the war not only lost the fight, but McCarthy also lost the nomination, and Hubert Humphrey was chosen as the Democrat candidate. Humphrey had been Vice President from 1964 while President Johnson was escalating the war. To gain enough votes to win the nomination, he had to have Johnson's support, which meant that he also had to accept Johnson's Vietnam policy. In the few weeks before the election, Humphrey tried to distance himself from Johnson's policies, but it was too late and Nixon won the election by a very narrow margin.

Economic troubles

Many American families were affected by the war through their sons being drafted, but soon all Americans were feeling the effects of the inflation that it caused. President Johnson had concealed the true cost of the war, saying in 1967 that it was costing $800 million a month. The true cost was closer to $2000 million a month, but Johnson thought that if this were known it would affect his plans for social change, his Great Society. He delayed an increase in taxes as long as possible, and did not ask Congress until mid-1967. Congress delayed any action for almost a year, before it approved a 10 per cent tax surcharge. By this time, the United States' budget deficit had increased from $10 billion to $30 billion, and inflation was climbing; '[t]he inflation spiral that was eventually to cripple the United States and the rest of the world had begun its dizzy ascent'.[9]

Opposition to the war on the grounds of its cost developed. By 1968, a US senator asked why the United States was spending $66 million per day 'trying to save the 16 million people of South Vietnam while leaving the plight of 20 million urban poor in the USA unresolved'.[10] The problems of America's cities became obvious when a wave of rioting spread through them after the assassination of Martin Luther King in April 1968. However money kept going to the war and not into aid for the cities.

Political costs

The Vietnam War destroyed Johnson's presidency. It was the major issue in the 1968 presidential election that Richard Nixon won with his promise to end the war.

The anti-war movement was largely responsible for the secrecy and paranoia that developed in Nixon's White House, and this suspicious, secretive atmosphere led on naturally to Watergate. President Nixon's Chief of Staff, H. R. Haldeman, has said that 'without the Vietnam War there would have been no Watergate'.[11] The Watergate scandal forced President Nixon to resign in 1974 and weakened the power and prestige of the presidency.

Vietnam caused a generation of Americans to distrust their government. They had been deceived by their presidents, especially Johnson and Nixon, and would be cautious about accepting the word of their powers that be in the future.

The Pentagon Papers

The extent to which the public had been deceived about the war was revealed in 1971 with the publication of the Pentagon Papers. In 1967, Secretary of Defense Robert McNamara was beginning to question the conduct of the war and requested that a top-secret history of United States' involvement in Indo China be prepared. One of his aides, Daniel Ellsberg, had a copy of the report made. For Ellsberg, the invasion of Laos in February 1971 was the last straw and he leaked the report to the *New York Times*, which proceeded to publish large extracts. President Johnson failed in his attempts to prevent publication through the courts and he then turned to illegal methods. He set up a group called the 'plumbers', who started their activities by breaking into the office of Ellsberg's psychiatrist, to try to gather material that would discredit Ellsberg. (The plumbers were also used by Nixon in 1972 to carry out the burglary of the Democratic Party headquarters in the Watergate building. This burglary set in train the events that led to Nixon's eventual resignation and disgrace.)

Review

- What were the social, political and economic effects of the war on the United States?
- How did opposition to the war in the US differ from opposition in Australia? How do you account for these differences?

Research

- Find out about some of the people involved in the anti-war movement: Dave Dellinger, Tom Hayden (who later married actor Jane Fonda), Jerry Rubin, Abbie Hoffman (died 1989).
- What music was associated with this movement? How did this music change from 1965 to 1973? You might start with the music from *Woodstock*.

THE INDO CHINA WAR

CHAPTER ELEVEN

1969–1975

NIXON'S VIETNAM POLICY

PRESIDENT NIXON'S election promise on Vietnam was that he would achieve 'peace with honour', but Nixon's view of peace was different from that of most Americans. According to Hugh Higgins, 'What President Nixon means by peace is what other people mean by victory'.[1] Nixon had no intention of being the first President to lose a war. He still intended to win, but by different means than those used by Johnson. His main policy of Vietnamisation meant that the fighting on the ground would be handed over to the ARVN, thus greatly lessening US casualties and making the war more acceptable to the American people. The United States would back up the South Vietnamese by supplying plenty of weapons and by giving them air support. Nixon would then be able to negotiate a peace settlement that would allow him to win the 1972 election.

Vietnamisation meant that US troop levels would start to decline, with 60 000 withdrawn during 1969. These withdrawals meant a change in military approach and an end to Search and Destroy missions. This suited the Communists who needed a chance to rebuild after the heavy losses of 1968. Gabriel Kolko reported that, 'Communist military activity was reduced to a level just high enough to keep the remaining enemy forces dispersed, provide aid to political efforts, and cause sufficient US casualties to sustain political pressure on the administration to continue troop withdrawals'.[2]

The Americans failed to develop such a clear strategy for their army while it was withdrawing. They tried pointless attacks such as Hamburger Hill to show that they were still in business, but these attacks only served to further weaken the US Army from within. As the soldiers became aware during 1969 that their job was to 'hold the fort until the Indians make peace', their only interest became survival and their motto was 'CYA (Cover Your Ass) and get

At Kent State University on 4 May 1970 a detachment of National Guardsmen, called in to put down a massive anti-war rally, were confronted by a large group of student protestors. Feeling threatened, the Guardsmen fired teargas and bullets into a crowd of about 500 students. Ten people were wounded and four killed. Why were the students protesting on this day? (UPI/Bettmann Newsphotos)

back home'.[3] Discipline in the army disintegrated, and racism and drugs became serious problems. By 1971, there was increasing pressure to get the Army out before it collapsed completely.

The American CIA (Central Intelligence Agency) and the South Vietnamese started the Phoenix Program during 1969 to weaken the Viet Cong's political support. The idea was to draw up centralised lists of suspected Viet Cong cadres and supporters and then have them arrested. South Vietnamese local officials were given quotas, and often filled their quota by arresting anyone they could find. Over half the people arrested bribed their way out, with the usual cost being $25 to $50. The system was also open to abuse as it could easily be used to remove opponents or settle grudges. Torture and executions

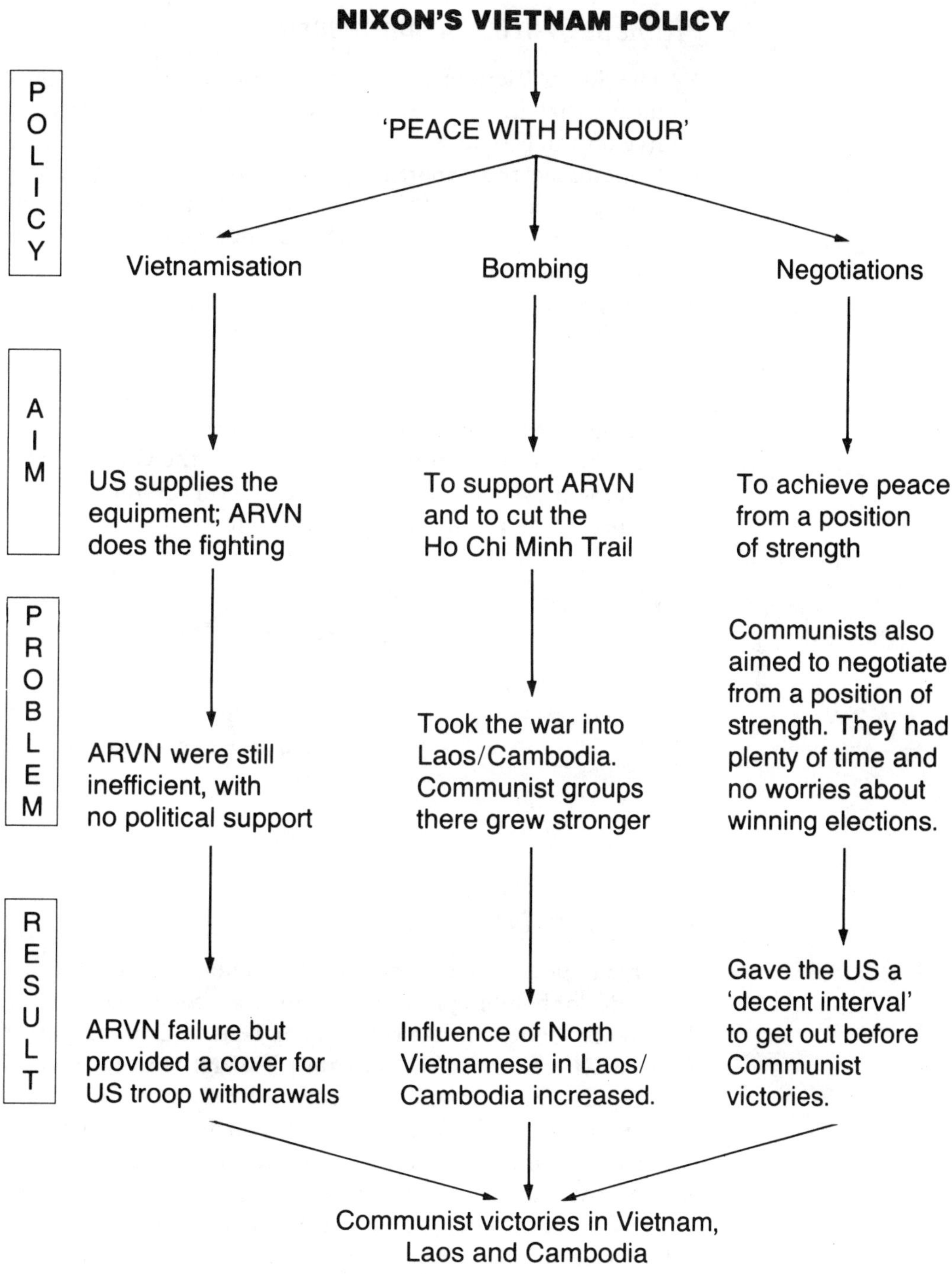

were common. Over 80 000 were arrested up to 1972, and an estimated 6000 killed. Stanley Karnow claims that the Phoenix Program was a real threat to the Viet Cong as it struck at the base of their power.[4] Other historians, such as Gabriel Kolko, stress that the program caused great controversy but are doubtful about its effectiveness.[5]

Problems with Vietnamisation

- The South Vietnamese Army was increased to over a million men. This meant that there were twice as many soldiers to drain the economy and live off the people.
- It increased the opportunities for officers to take part in corruption. The example was set at the top, with Vice President Nguyen Cao Ky playing a central role in the drug trade. Making money and playing politics occupied most of the general's time.
- The US became closely tied to the Thieu regime. This small group lacked political support and relied on the Army to stay in power.
- The ARVN became reliant on US weapons (M–16s, Hueys, tanks). The ARVN were not familiar with these weapons and they were not weapons that had been successful for the US in the war.
- The military initiative was clearly with the Communists. The North Vietnamese played an increasing role and the Communist Army became much more a regular army than a guerrilla force.

Review

- What was meant by Vietnamisation?
- Why was it likely to fail?

Discuss

What similarities were there between the situation in 1969–1970 and the situation towards the end of the Diem regime (1960–1963)?

Escalation, Nixon-style

In March 1969, two months after he came to power, Nixon approved the first of a series of bombing raids on Cambodia, code-named Operation Menu. Nixon incorrectly believed that there was a central Communist headquarters called Central Office for South Vietnam (COSVN) located in the Fish Hook region, just inside the Cambodian border. The Cambodian Prime Minister, Prince Norodom Sihanouk, had given approval for the Americans to pursue Communists across the border, but had not approved B–52 bombing raids. Nixon ordered total secrecy for these raids, and the American people found out about them four years later. Air Force records of the raids were falsified, and the telephones of some White House officials and reporters were tapped. The bombing continued through 1969, but all it achieved was to push the Communist troops further into Cambodia, and to create many refugees.

By early 1970, Nixon was frustrated at the lack of progress in the peace negotiations, and wanted to put pressure on North Vietnam and the Soviet Union. His opportunity came in March 1970 when Prince Sihanouk was overthrown and replaced by the pro-American Lon Nol. Nixon had just announced the withdrawal of a further 150 000 troops during 1970, and wanted to show that, despite Vietnamisation, the United States was still strong and committed to stopping the Communists. In a televised speech to the American people on 30 April, he announced that:

> “Tonight, American and South Vietnamese units will attack the headquarters of the entire Communist operations in South Vietnam. This key control centre has been occupied by North Vietnamese and Viet Cong for five years in blatant violation of Cambodia's neutrality. The operation will protect US forces in Vietnam.”

Fifteen thousand American and 5000 ARVN troops crossed the border into Cambodia. Prime Minister Lon Nol was not consulted. Over the next two months they pushed 30 kilometres into Cambodia before withdrawing. No COSVN-type headquarters were found, but large numbers of supplies and weapons were seized. The main effect, however, was that 200 000 refugees fled into Cambodia. The Communists moved with them, and civil war rapidly developed. The Cambodian Communists, the Khmer Rouge, had not been an important force, but they now gained support from North Vietnam and the Viet Cong as well as from supporters of Sihanouk. They grew rapidly and within a few months controlled most of the Cambodian countryside. Nixon's invasion had increased the power of the Khmer Rouge and set in train the future destruction of the Cambodian people.

LAOS, 1945–1975

When the French returned to Laos after World War II, two separate resistance movements against their rule developed. The Lao Issara (Free Lao) wanted independence for Laos under a monarchy, while the Pathet Lao wanted Communist control and worked closely with the Viet Minh. The Geneva Conference in 1954, which followed the defeat of the French in Vietnam, granted full independence to Laos but did not settle the issue of who was to rule.

Over the next few years, there were a number of unsuccessful attempts to set up a coalition government to bring the royalists and Communists together. Fighting broke out in 1960 between the Royal Lao Army and the Pathet Lao, but was settled when another Geneva Conference in May 1961 set up a neutral, independent government, led by Prince Souvanna Phouma. Both Kennedy and Khrushchev guaranteed the neutrality of Laos, and it was thought for a while that the Laotian solution could also be used in Vietnam. However, this did not happen and the events in Vietnam started to threaten Laotian neutrality. In 1964, as the Ho Chi Minh Trail became a vital link for the Viet Cong, the United States started secret bombing raids on the trail. These raids were directed from the US embassy in Laos, and used old American planes with Royal Lao markings.[6] North Vietnam increased its support for the Pathet Lao, who rapidly gained control of large areas of the countryside.

President Nixon's Vietnamisation policy spread the war further into Laos, and led to increased bombing raids on the Ho Chi Minh Trail. In early 1971, Nixon wanted to gain more time for the South Vietnamese Government by cutting off supplies along the trail. This time the Communists knew of the plan, and the ARVN soldiers fell into a well prepared trap when they invaded Laos in February 1971. The plan was for 17000 ARVN troops to advance into Laos, with US air and artillery support. They managed to advance 30 kilometres before the trap was sprung. Estimates of ARVN soldiers killed range from 3500 to 9000. Four hundred Americans were killed, and up to 700 US planes and helicopters destroyed.

This invasion (Operation Lam Son 719) was supposed to be a crucial test of the Vietnamisation policy. Instead it exposed the weakness of the ARVN, and its inability to co-ordinate a large attack. The attack also strengthened the North Vietnamese influence in Laos. Two years later, when the Americans finally withdrew from South Vietnam, an agreement was signed for Laos that led to the formation of a coalition government. This time, the coalition was heavily dominated by the Communist Pathet Lao, which in turn was dominated by the North Vietnamese. In 1975, the Pathet Lao took complete control of the government, and set up the Lao People's Democratic Republic.

Review

- Why did Nixon attack Cambodia and Laos?
- How did the Vietnam War become the Indo China War?
- How did the invasions strengthen the positions of the Communists in both countries?

THE 1972 OFFENSIVE

The Communists had staged no major attacks up to 1972, preferring to hold the line while they rebuilt their forces. By March 1972 they were ready to test the success of Vietnamisation, and to put pressure on Nixon at the start of an election year. They also wanted to improve their negotiating position in Paris. On 30 March, 140 000 North Vietnamese troops attacked three major positions: the North provinces, the Central Highlands, and the Mekong Delta. The main attack was a conventional military attack across the DMZ, supported by 500 Soviet tanks and artillery. This caused tremendous confusion in the ARVN, and one of their two divisions panicked and fled. The NVA captured the important provincial capital of Quang Tri, and held it until September. They also threatened the old capital of Hué, but their advances were slowed down by massive US air and naval power which gave the ARVN some time to regroup. The United States also responded by mining the harbour of Haiphong. The 1972 Spring Offensive showed that:

- The South Vietnamese Government only survived because of United States support.
- Vietnamisation had failed.
- The ARVN was led by incompetents and discipline was poor.
- The North Vietnamese could not achieve a military victory. Like the Americans, they would have to turn to diplomacy.

PEACE NEGOTIATIONS

Following President Johnson's withdrawal from the presidential race, peace talks began in Paris in May 1968. There were problems from the start. The NLF and ARVN refused to recognise each other, and it took seven months to work out suitable seating arrangements. Once the talking began, the North Vietnamese took a consistent approach, insisting that the United States had to withdraw first to allow the two Vietnams to reach an agreement. In May 1969, Henry Kissinger (Nixon's special negotiator in Paris), suggested that both sides withdraw. The South Vietnamese rejected this idea, and showed that they would be more difficult in the negotiations than the North Vietnamese. The South wanted to guarantee its survival after a US withdrawal, whereas Kissinger only wanted a suitable agreement to cover the withdrawal. Partly to get around the South Vietnamese, Kissinger and the North Vietnamese representative, Le Duc Tho, started a series of secret meetings in August 1969.

No real progress was made in either the official or secret talks during 1970 and 1971. The Communists were in no hurry, knowing that time was on their side. Nixon had to face an election at the end of 1972 and the invasions of Laos and Cambodia had achieved nothing, either militarily or politically. He now realised that he could not achieve a military victory and would have to negotiate a settlement. (Nixon also had other things on his mind. In 1972 he visited Beijing as a sign of the rapidly improving relations between China and the US. It was also a sign of the declining relations between China and North Vietnam.)

Negotiations in Paris became more serious and in October 1972 a ceasefire agreement was reached between Le Duc Tho and Kissinger. Some of the provisions of the agreement were:

- Thieu would remain as President of South Vietnam. The Communists dropped their demand for a coalition government.

Bruce Petty, the Australian, *17 August 1972, courtesy of Bruce Petty*

- American troops would be withdrawn and US bases closed.
- The South would continue to receive US military aid.
- 150 000 NVA troops would remain in the South.

However President Thieu refused to accept the provisions of the agreement and the talks collapsed.

President Nixon then lashed out and ordered the saturation bombing of Haiphong and Hanoi. From 18–30 December the bombing continued twenty-four hours a day, except for Christmas Day, and a total of 100 000 bombs were dropped. The purpose of the attacks was not to influence the North but to demonstrate to Thieu that he could count on US support, even after troop withdrawal.

On 23 January 1973 the Paris peace agreement was finally signed, the same agreement that had been negotiated in October and basically the same as the one that could have been reached in 1970. Few people believed that the settlement would last but it gave the Americans what they wanted — a decent interval to get out before the South collapsed. The last US soldiers left in March and the ARVN Government lasted another two years.

Review

- Why did both sides get more serious about negotiating in 1972? Why did it take so long?
- Why was the agreement not likely to last?

Discuss

- As a role-playing exercise, take the part of the various representatives at the peace conference in mid-1972. What would your minimum and maximum demands be? What arguments would you use?
- According to the cartoon what was Nixon's attitude to the peace negotiations?

NIXON'S FALL

After the last American troops left Vietnam in March 1973, the US public tried to forget about Vietnam. President Nixon, however, had been re-elected in November 1972 with a huge majority, and came back into office more arrogant than ever. He had assured President Thieu that he would be supported, and the resumption of the bombing of Hanoi was a strong possibility. The United States Congress was aware of Nixon's attitude, but was now determined to stand up to him and passed a law forbidding any US bombing attacks in Indo China after 15 August. Nixon was also under increasing pressure during 1973 as the Watergate scandal developed and his past deceptions caught up with him. The events of 1973 and 1974 developed as follows:

April 1973: Nixon's aides (H. R. Haldeman, John Ehrlichman and John Dean) resigned over charges of their involvement in the burglary of the Democratic Party headquarters.

June 1973: Nixon was accused by Dean of attempting to cover up the Watergate burglary.

October 1973: Vice President Spiro Agnew was forced to resign over charges that he accepted bribes.

May 1974: House Judiciary Committee began impeachment hearings against President Nixon.

July 1974: The Committee recommended that Nixon be impeached.

9 August 1974: Nixon resigned. Gerald Ford became President.

With Nixon's decline and fall, United States support for Thieu also declined. In early 1974, Nixon had promised $2 billion in military aid each year, but with his departure this figure was trimmed to $700 million for 1975 with only $300 million being spent. President Ford was clearly not committed to Thieu. The North Vietnamese were aware that the situation had changed and at the end of 1974 started planning a large offensive for 1976.

Both the economy of South Vietnam and its Army had become dependent on massive amounts of American aid. When this aid dried up during 1973 both were greatly affected, and support for Thieu's Government fell even further. Many Vietnamese in the cities had been reliant on US money, and urban unemployment rose to over 30 per cent while income fell by almost 50 per cent. South Vietnam's balance of trade was disastrous, with imports exceeding exports by more than ten to one. Inflation rose rapidly, particularly with the worldwide inflation crisis at the end of 1973, when Arab countries suddenly quadrupled the price of oil. Corruption reached new peaks, as generals and top officials took advantage of the chaos. Thieu tried to keep control by tightening his police state. He admitted to having 30 000 political prisoners, but the real number probably exceeded 100 000.

During the war against the Viet Minh twenty-five years earlier, the French had been unable to set up a government with wide popular support. This situation had not changed with the Americans, who kept supporting governments that represented only a small section of the population, and which failed to carry out the reforms the majority of the people wanted. Democracy was forgotten and elections controlled to ensure a favourable result. Thieu won the presidential election of 1971 with money from the American CIA. America had created a South Vietnam whose economy, society and political system depended on US support. When that support dried up during 1973–1974, it was left with a shattered economy, a confused society and a political system that only survived through repression and that lacked popular support.

Review

- Why did American support for South Vietnam decline during 1973–1974?
- What effect did this have on the country?

Discuss

- What sections of the population would have been most affected by the withdrawal of US support?
- Why was Nixon forced to resign?

THE FINAL OFFENSIVE

In late 1974, the Communist leadership decided that the time was right to try to reunify Vietnam within two years. They were regaining control of the villages in the south and they knew that the RVN Government had little support. The ARVN had held the military situation for two years but the costs had been high. Casualties had been running at more than 1000 per month, and its supplies were being used up and not replaced. It also lacked the US bombing and helicopter support that had been so valuable in previous battles. The Communists were also confident that the United States would not intervene this time.

In January 1975, they sent a small force of 8000 NVA into Phuoc Long province, about 100 kilometres north of Saigon, to test the situation. They easily captured the province, and the US did nothing except to issue a diplomatic protest. The Communist leaders then decided to step up the schedule. General Van Tien Dung, described by Karnow as 'one of the few authentic peasants'[7] in the Communist leadership, had replaced General Giap as chief Communist strategist and was smuggled into the South to direct the final offensive.

This offensive was launched on 1 March and within ten days the NVA had captured the major Central Highlands town of Ban Me Thuot. President Thieu decided to abandon most of the northern area to the Communists, and ordered the evacuation of the towns of Kontum and Pleiku. His plan was to concentrate his forces around the northern coastal cities and in the south. Instead, it created panic as hundreds of thousands of refugees desperately tried to reach the coast. This chaotic situation was made worse when Hué was captured on 25 March. General Dung then sent 35 000 troops to surround

The final days of the war, culminating in the fall of Saigon to Communist forces

the 3 million people who had crowded into Da Nang, and who were supposedly protected by 100 000 ARVN. The people tried desperately to escape, some by racing up the airstrip on scooters to try to catch the last plane. Many of them were aware of the execution of thousands by the Communists when they captured Hué in February 1968, and expected a similar bloodbath. The Americans cancelled plans for a mass evacuation because of the panic. On 30 March, the Communists took over the city, capturing 100 000 leaderless troops. Their leaders had fled earlier.

Hanoi now stepped up plans to capture Saigon before the wet season began in May, and before Thieu could reorganise his troops. By 21 April they had surrounded Saigon and the Americans started to fly out non-essential Americans and their dependants.

> It seemed that anyone could go, as long as he, or more usually she, was 'sponsored' by an American. Familiar faces of whores from Tu Do Street appeared in the crush, affecting demure expressions and wearing Barbie-doll dresses . . . There was a faster, almost VIP procedure for another category of 'high risk' passenger. President Ford had called these people 'endangered Vietnamese'; they were all murderers . . . All of them had worked, at one time or another, for the CIA's Phoenix Programme: 'programme' being the euphemism for death squad.

John Pilger, *Heroes*, Pan, London, 1986, pp. 204–5

By 29 April the airport had been cut off as the Communist troops moved into the suburbs. The US embassy ordered the evacuation, and over the next eighteen hours moved 6000 people by helicopter to US ships off Saigon. President Thieu had left Saigon four days earlier and was replaced by 'Big Minh'. At 10.00 a.m. on 30 April Minh announced over the radio:

> I believe firmly in reconciliation among all Vietnamese. To avoid needless bloodshed, I ask the soldiers of the Republic to put an end to all hostilities. Be calm and remain where you are now. To save the lives of the people, do not open fire.
>
> I also call on our brothers, the soldiers of the Provisional Revolutionary Government, not to open fire, because we are waiting here to meet with their representatives to discuss the orderly turnover of the reins of government.

Quoted in Bowden, *One Crowded Hour*, pp. 331–2

A US crewman helps people climb a ladder to a waiting helicopter from a building rooftop during the evacuation of Saigon on 29 April 1975. American and foreign nationals were evacuated to waiting US Navy ships off the coast (photo by Van Es, UPI)

Above *The fall of the presidential palace, Saigon, 30 April 1975. These North Vietnamese tanks arrived in front of the palace where General Minh was waiting for them (Buffon-Darquenne/ Sygma, courtesy of John Hillelson Agency Limited)*

At 11.30 a.m. Australian cameraman Neil Davis waited in the grounds of the presidential palace as the Communist tanks arrived.

“I started to film as that tank, No 843, smashed through the front gates of Independence Palace.

It didn't quite make it the first time, and one gate fell off its hinges. It backed off and smashed through again, and this time both gates broke wide open. The soldier on the front holding the huge Viet Cong flag jumped off and ran towards the palace, and I followed him with my sound camera rolling.”

Davis was approached by an aggressive Communist soldier:

“And I did keep filming until he got right up to me and poked me in the guts with his rifle, screaming, 'Stop... hands up!'

Then I did stop, and put my hands up, still holding my fifteen-pound [6.8 kilogram] sound camera in my right hand, so I couldn't keep my hands up for very long. As quickly as I could, I got off my Vietnamese welcoming speech, which was, 'Welcome to Saigon, comrade. I've been waiting for you.'”

Bowden, *One Crowded Hour*, p. 338. Also in the film *Frontline*

Neil Davis's camera was rolling when North Vietnamese tank No. 843 smashed through the gates of Saigon's presidential palace on 30 April 1975. It was a symbolic moment for the North Vietnamese: the reunification of the two Vietnams (© Tim Bowden & Neil Davis, One Crowded Hour, *courtesy Collins/Angus & Robertson)*

Review

- Why were the Communists able to take over the South so quickly?
- What effects did these events have:
  - (a) Invasion of Cambodia, 30 April 1970
  - (b) Lam Son 719 campaign, February 1971
  - (c) Paris peace agreement, 27 January 1973
  - (d) Nixon's resignation, 9 August 1974
  - (e) Communist capture of Ban Me Thuot, 11 March 1975

Research

- What was happening in Cambodia and Laos during April 1975?
- Did a bloodbath follow the Communist takeover?

Structured questions

- What was President Nixon's Vietnamisation policy?
- How did this policy turn the Vietnam War into the Indo China War?
- How did the failure of Vietnamisation lead to Communist victories throughout Indo China?

AFTERMATH OF WAR

Focus question

How have the lives of the Vietnamese people changed under Communist rule?

(a) How did each of the following aspects of life change: education, industry, housing, jobs, culture, social classes?

(b) Which groups in Vietnam have suffered most under Communist rule?

(c) Which groups have gained under Communism? Has the struggle of the war been worth it?

Courtesy of Don Wright, Miami News

'Thanks a lot'

Control by the North

When the Communist troops moved into Saigon in April 1975, the Provisional Revolutionary Government moved in with them, expecting to take over the government of South Vietnam. Truong Nhu Tang was with them, but found that taking over as Minister of Justice would be difficult. The North Vietnamese were determined to show from the start that victory meant victory for the North, and that unification meant control by the North.

> "In the days that followed, I became aware that our police and security were being handled exclusively by various DRV (North Vietnam) Departments. Now that I thought about it, I realized that all the arrangements for the victory celebration had also been taken care of by the DRV. We all began to note the extent to which Northern cadres were filling positions of responsibility on our staffs and handling business of every variety."

Truong Nhu Tang, *A Vietcong Memoir*, p. 265

Tang also observed that re-education camps were set up, and that he, as Minister of Justice, had no control over these camps. He was told that people would only be in the camps for a month, so he drove his two brothers to one of the camps. Tang soon discovered that the month was the minimum, and most people stayed for years. One of his brothers was still in a camp in 1985.

Re-education camps

Mr Ngo H had fought in the ARVN. In the following interview, from the Oral History Collection in the National Library, he discusses his experiences.

> In June [1975], they [the Communists] declared that all former officers had to present themselves and go to re-education camp. At the time, they told us that we only needed to bring food for 10 days. After that, we would be returned to our families... I decided to go and present myself to the communist government and study in re-education camps as I had been told.
>
> 'Re-education camp' was only a name the communists used. In reality it was a jail. For over 4 or 5 years we didn't study anything; we were just labourers, and extremely miserable. The work exhausted people. People who returned seemed to be unbalanced in their minds, to have no memory, to be tense or perhaps mad...

- What was the purpose of the re-education camps? What people were likely to have been seen as needing 're-education'? What other actions were taken against such people?

Education

Miss Nguyen now lives in Sydney, having escaped from Vietnam in 1984. Her father had been a police officer who was sent to a re-education camp in 1975 for 7 years. She had to falsify her personal records to be accepted at Teacher's College, because, as a 'puppet (regime) child' she would not normally be accepted. At college, she found that she was part of the 'Communist brainwashing system'.

> Before brainwashing the students you have to first brainwash the teachers, because the teacher is the implement for instructing the students. Right there in the teacher's college my own teachers had already been brainwashed.

She found, once she was sent teaching, that there were distinct groups of students in her class. Miss Nguyen called the main groups the passives and the opposites.

> Usually the passive ones in the class were the children of the 'puppet' group associated with the Republic of Vietnam. The student was passive in class because he was embarrassed because he was not allowed to participate in the new society...
>
> On the other hand there were the students who were the opposite... Usually these children turn out to be from families who worked for the revolution, or they could be the children of 'heroes'. The children of 'heroes' have priority for advancement to the next grade and must have priority for Grade A results for 'Virtue', so they don't fear the teacher.

Interview with Miss Nguyen, Oral History Collection, National Library

Because of this, they were difficult and Miss Nguyen would visit their homes to find out why. She discovered that usually they were from the homes of 'heroes' who were resentful that they had not been fully rewarded for their part in the victory — these people had expected to get the best land from land reform.

Vietnamese students, Ho Chi Minh City. Many girls now wear the traditional ao dai *costume to school, particularly in the South. Despite Communist efforts to control education, students show increasing independence and are more interested in pop stars than in Ho Chi Minh*

- How were the students to be brainwashed?
- Which group of students did Miss Nguyen find to be the most difficult? Why?
- What indications of disenchantment with Communism are there in her story?

Industry

Mr Ho Van Hieu was an industrialist before 1975, and was allowed to continue operating for a while under Communist rule because he was useful to the new regime.

> “After the Communists came I was classified as a so-called industrial bourgeois because most of my close relatives earned their living by working at factories, repairing auto machines and so on... After the Communist take-over, I was very afraid and had to find another job so as to avoid their suspicious eyes. That was why I established a co-operative called Minh Ha of which I was manager. [Mr Ho's factory built prefabricated houses.]
>
> It was not until 1981, no, November 1980, that the 9th Military Region Headquarters received instructions from the Defence Department to buy out my factory. All my property was inventoried and sealed off. The whole factory was then worth 233,000 dong. I brought along with me to Bidong [Pilau Bidong — a refugee camp in Malaysia] a bill of debt issued by the Viet Cong certifying that they owed me 233,000 dong.”

Interview with Mr Ho Van Hieu, Oral History Collection, National Library

Discuss

- Why was Mr Ho allowed to continue as an industrialist? How did this conflict with Communist ideology?
- Why did the Communists decide to take over his factory in 1980?
- Why were people put in categories, such as 'industrial bourgeois', after 1975? What other categories would there have been?

Literature

Mrs Nguyen Van Son was a well known journalist in Vietnam who left in 1980. She said that she left for two reasons:

> "1 I couldn't bear to bow my head and become a lackey for the Communists. I am old and infirm now; if I stayed behind to resist them I had no means to do so, no means at all.
> 2 My second aim was to join with our fellow countrymen in the community, to eradicate the weeds of Communism once they sprout here in Australia."

Mrs Nguyen was asked how culture in a free democratic country was different from that under a Communist regime.

> "Ah! The differences are like chalk and cheese. Everyone should know that! If you were a writer under a free regime, you can write what you like... But with the Vietnamese Communists... and I'm certain it holds true for all Communist countries, writers all have to live in a controlled cultural environment. I myself have experienced it. They asked me to write for the newspaper *Giai-Phong* [Liberation] in Saigon. They gave me the topics to write on, and for each article they would have paid me 6 dong. If I wanted to write a book, they would give me the topics on which I could write."

Interview with Mrs Nguyen Van Son, Oral History Collection, National Library

- What does Mrs Nguyen mean by 'eradicate the weeds of Communism' in Australia?
- Why did the Communists want a 'controlled cultural environment'? Apart from writers, what other groups would be controlled?

Each of the people whose stories appear in this section, 'Aftermath of war', have escaped from Vietnam. Each of them had clear reasons for hating the Communist system enough to flee their home country.

- What were these reasons?
- How do the interviewees show their attitudes in their accounts?
- Does this make them less reliable as observers of life in Vietnam?
- Would some people who still live in Vietnam share any of their reasons for disliking the Communist system?
- How would you find out what the people who live there think?

CAMBODIA

CHAPTER TWELVE

IN THE TWELFTH CENTURY, when the vast Angkor Wat temple complex was built, Cambodia was the centre of an empire that included most of Southern Vietnam, Laos, Thailand and parts of Malaya. In the centuries that followed, this empire was broken up as the Thais expanded from the west, and then the Vietnamese pushed the Khmers out of Vietnam. By the time the French arrived in the mid-nineteenth century, the Cambodians welcomed French protection to prevent their country being broken up even more. These struggles left the Cambodians deeply distrustful of both their neighbours, particularly the Vietnamese, and with a desire to reclaim the southern part of Vietnam, which they continued to call Kampuchea Krom.

In 1941, the French chose the 18-year-old Prince Norodom Sihanouk to be king. Sihanouk already had a reputation as a playboy, and the French assumed that this would make him easier to manipulate. However, there was more substance to Sihanouk than there was to Bao Dai in Vietnam. During the Viet Minh's war against the French, Sihanouk largely kept his country out of it, although a number of Cambodian Communists did fight with the Viet Minh. Instead, Sihanouk staged a worldwide publicity campaign that forced the French to grant independence in 1953, a year before the Viet Minh victory at Dien Bien Phu. This undermined the Communists, as Sihanouk had gained independence without them.

In 1955, Sihanouk abdicated as king to enter politics. He formed his own political party and was appointed head of state after an easy election victory. Sihanouk was enormously popular throughout Cambodia, particularly amongst the peasants who treated him as if he were one of the god-kings from Cambodia's past period of greatness.[1] He was all things to the people: song-writer, poet, film director and star, soccer player. He was not a military dictator, and the Army was kept small and divided. Sihanouk set out to improve health and education facilities. Cities began to develop rapidly and became a magnet for the newly educated people. These people were attracted to American-style consumerism, but others became increasingly repelled by what they saw as the corruption of the cities.

Sihanouk tried throughout to follow a neutral policy. At home, he attempted to keep a balance between the left and right wings, whilst in foreign policy he tried to avoid entanglement in the Vietnam War and to maintain good relations with the Chinese and the Americans. A small Communist group did develop in the jungles, where it gained some support from the hill tribes, but it was always harshly repressed by Sihanouk, who had no interest in Communism. In the cities, rapid growth depended on foreign aid, and, up to 1963, Sihanouk accepted aid from both the United States and the Communist countries. This frustrated the United States, which tended to equate neutrality with pro-Communism, and there are suggestions that from 1959 the CIA was trying to undermine Sihanouk.

After the assassination of Ngo Dinh Diem in November 1963, Sihanouk ordered the Americans out of Cambodia and refused to accept American aid. Sihanouk was not impressed with the way in which America treated its friends, such as Diem. He also became convinced that the Communists would win in Vietnam, and that he should stay on good terms with them. Sihanouk started to develop closer ties with China, as he knew that China would protect Cambodia if Vietnam became too powerful. From 1965, he also allowed the Vietnamese Communists to set up bases inside Cambodia, and to bring some of their supplies through the Cambodian port of Sihanoukville. In return, the Communists would respect Cambodian borders after they won.

This anti-American stance and tolerance of Communism greatly increased opposition to Sihanouk. Many people were affected by the lack of US aid, particularly the Army officers who were missing out on their side-benefits. In 1967, Sihanouk tried to balance this up by appointing General Lon Nol as Prime Minister. One of his first acts was a harsh put-down of a peasant revolt in the western province of Battambang. This led to repression in the cities which forced many left-wingers, such as Khieu Samphan, to join the Communists in the jungle. Sihanouk labelled them the Khmer Rouge. Sihanouk also tried to rebuild relations with the United States, and when President Nixon began the secret bombing of Cambodia in March 1969 he did not protest. When the bombing started, the Khmer Rouge had only 4000 members, but this number rapidly increased as the bombing forced the Communists deeper into Cambodia.

Concern within Cambodia at the presence of an estimated 40 000 Vietnamese Communists reached a peak in early 1970, just when Sihanouk decided on an overseas holiday. During his absence, protests against the Vietnamese grew rapidly and became violent. These protests were encouraged by Lon Nol who took the opportunity on 18 March to overthrow Sihanouk and take full power himself. The United States immediately recognised the Lon Nol Government. Sihanouk was trapped in Beijing, from where he announced the formation of a National United Front and called on his supporters to go to the jungle and fight as guerrillas. In effect, this was a declaration of support for the Khmer Rouge. Lon Nol's coup had ended Sihanouk's neutrality and forced him to turn to the Chinese and the Khmer Rouge for support. Lon Nol was strongly anti-Communist, and gave them an ultimatum to leave Cambodia within

Phnom Penh, the capital of Cambodia, came under heavy attack in early 1975 as Communist forces moved in. The body of a civilian lies beside his burning motorcycle on the main street after Communist rebels fired eighteen rockets into the city. Thirteen were killed and thirty-four wounded (UPI, courtesy Popperfoto)

seventy-two hours. This was a virtual declaration of war, as the Vietnamese had no intention of leaving their bases, but it was a war that the weak Cambodian Army was not prepared for.

The Communists easily pushed the Cambodian Army aside and took over the areas they needed to give them access to Vietnam. President Nixon then entered the scene on 30 April 1970, when he announced the invasion of Cambodia by US and ARVN troops to destroy Communist bases. This forced the Communists to retreat further from the border areas and go deeper into Cambodia. Support for the Khmer Rouge increased amongst the Cambodian peasants who were increasingly disturbed by the US bombing and by the actions of the ARVN troops. Civil war developed and by July 1970 the Khmer Rouge, with North Vietnamese support, occupied over half the country. Hundreds of thousands of refugees headed for the capital, Phnom Penh.

Lon Nol abolished the monarchy in October 1970, and set up the Khmer Republic with himself as President. It was a republic that controlled little more than the areas around Phnom Penh and Battambang and the road between the two. It relied for survival on a corrupt and inefficient army containing a large number of boy soldiers. Survival increasingly depended on US bombing, but this was stopped by Congress in August 1973, just after the bombing of Neak Luong, shown in the film *The Killing Fields*. Lon Nol had virtually no understanding of international affairs, and as the war intensified and his country's economy crumbled, he seemed oblivious to Cambodia's predicament. His government was corrupt and inefficient and, largely because of its reliance on the United States, hated by the people. Defeat at the hands of the Khmer Rouge seemed increasingly inevitable, but Lon Nol remained immovable as the economy disintegrated, refugees flooded into Phnom Penh, and his army stumbled from one setback to another. On 1 April 1975, with the Khmer Rouge rocketing Phnom Penh, Lon Nol left Cambodia. Seventeen days later the Khmer Rouge took over the city. Many felt relief that the war was over but this relief was short-lived.

Review

- Why was Sihanouk overthrown?
- How did this change the situation in Cambodia?
- How did the following events help the Khmer Rouge: the Battambang revolt, the secret bombing, and the invasion of 1970?

Discuss

- Should Sihanouk be criticised for failing, or praised for keeping Cambodia out of the war for so long?
- The following opinion of events in Cambodia was given by Neil Davis. Are his criticisms of Nixon and Kissinger justified?

> "The Cambodian people did not want to be involved in the war at all; the Americans dragged them in. President Nixon and his national security adviser Henry Kissinger were mainly responsible for Cambodia entering the war. Of course the Viet Cong and the North Vietnamese had sanctuaries in eastern Cambodia, and the Americans had wanted to wipe those out for a long while. They thought that by dragging Cambodia into the war on their side, they would eventually win the war in Indo-China. The only thing they were successful in doing was almost totally destroying twelve hundred years of Cambodian culture and civilisation, and the Cambodian people.
>
> Of course President Nixon and Henry Kissinger were deeply involved in the secret bombing of Cambodia in 1969, a totally illegal act in which many Cambodian civilians, and very few Communist troops, were killed.
>
> I believe that the actions of President Nixon and Henry Kissinger in dragging Cambodia into the war were criminal."

Bowden, *One Crowded Hour*, pp. 227–8

POL POT AND THE KHMER ROUGE

The Khmer Rouge leaders who took power in April 1975 were a group of urban intellectuals who had been attracted to Marxism whilst students in Paris in the early 1950s. Pol Pot was the most important of these, along with Ieng Sary and Khieu Samphan. By the early 1960s they had returned to Phnom Penh, mostly to take up jobs as teachers. They became involved in the Khmer Rouge and managed to change it from a peasant party to a workers' party. Pol Pot became Party Secretary in 1963, and in 1966 he visited China where he observed the Cultural Revolution at first hand. Like the others, Pol Pot

Once looked on by the Cambodian people as a god-king, Prince Sihanouk lost considerable support because of his coalition with the hated Khmer Rouge (The Age)

Far right. *Pol Pot, leader of the obsessively secretive and fanatical guerrilla group, the Khmer Rouge* (The Age)

embraced the Chinese style of Communism, and he was impressed by the mass mobilisation and the fanaticism of the Cultural Revolution.

The Khmer Rouge remained an insignificant force in Cambodia until Lon Nol's coup.

Following Lon Nol's coup, the situation in Cambodia changed very rapidly. Within weeks, the North Vietnamese Communist forces had taken control of all the areas that they needed to control the supply lines to Vietnam. They also gave much support to Pol Pot's Khmer Rouge. Sihanouk was obsessed with the idea that he was Cambodia's only hope, and he formed a United Front with the Khmer Rouge to oppose Lon Nol. The support of both North Vietnam and Sihanouk helped the Khmer Rouge to grow rapidly, and by 1972 they controlled most of Cambodia. Pol Pot then turned against both these supporters, first purging the Khmer Rouge of all Vietnamese influence, and then pushing out Sihanouk and his supporters.

In April 1975, having finally captured Phnom Penh, the Khmer Rouge took over control of the country they now called 'Democratic Kampuchea'. Prince Sihanouk, who had been living in Beijing since 1973, was persuaded to return to Phnom Penh as a figurehead leader of the new country, to try and give the Khmer Rouge more respectability. However, the Khmer Rouge held all the power, with the main leaders being Pol Pot, Khieu Samphan, Ieng Sary and Son Sen. Sihanouk realised he was being used, and resigned in April 1976. The Khmer Rouge placed him under house arrest. Except for two sons, all of Sihanouk's children and grandchildren were killed by the Khmer Rouge.

Review

- Why did the Khmer Rouge turn against both the Vietnamese and Sihanouk?

THE KILLING FIELDS, 1975–1978

Most people in Phnom Penh knew little about the Khmer Rouge when they marched in on 17 April. Neil Davis was one person who had no illusions:

> "I had no doubts there would be a bloodbath one way or the other. I didn't, however, envisage the total evacuation of Phnom Penh's three million people.
>
> I did know that the Cambodian Communists were not at all like their fellow-countrymen on the other side. They were a xenophobic clique of disenchanted radical so-called intellectuals, some of whom had graduated in France and other countries. But they had always been on the outside as far as the urban Cambodian people were concerned.
>
> They had a vitriolic hatred of the Cambodian people because of their earlier rejections, and they disliked the Vietnamese — including the Communists — because they had earlier rejected them also. It was only the American involvement which moved the Chinese and Vietnamese Communists to support them. That is how they found themselves in a position to take over the government."

Bowden, *One Crowded Hour*, pp. 314–15

Review

- What type of people were the Khmer Rouge? Who supported them? Why? Compare them to the Viet Cong.
- Why was such a group able to take power in Cambodia?

DOCUMENT STUDY

The Khmer Rouge

Read the following documents carefully and try to establish what the main ideas behind the ideology of the Khmer Rouge were. How did these ideas develop? How quickly did they carry out their policies?

Orders from Khmer Rouge leaders

> "**1** Evacuate people from all towns.
> **2** Abolish all markets.
> **3** Withdraw the Lon Nol currency, but withhold the revolutionary currency which had been printed.
> **4** Defrock all Buddhist monks, and put them to work growing rice.
> **5** Execute all leaders of the Lon Nol regime, beginning with the top leaders.
> **6** Establish high-level cooperatives throughout the country, with communal eating.
> **7** Expel the entire Vietnamese minority population.
> **8** Despatch troops to the country's borders, particularly the border with Vietnam."

Martin Stuart-Fox, *The Murderous Revolution*, Alternative Publishing Co-operative, Chippendale, 1985, pp. 33–4

> “*Cambodia Reds are uprooting millions as they impose a 'peasant revolution'*
>
> BANGKOK, THAILAND, MAY 8 — The victorious Cambodian Communists, who marched into Phnom Penh on April 17 and ended five years of war in Cambodia, are carrying out a peasant revolution that has thrown the entire country into upheaval.
>
> Perhaps as many as three or four million people, most of them on foot, have been forced out of the cities and sent on a mammoth and gruelling exodus into areas deep in the countryside where, the Communists say, they will have to become peasants and till the soil.
>
> No one has been excluded — even the very old, the very young, the sick and the wounded have been forced out onto the roads and some will clearly not be strong enough to survive.
>
> The old economy of the cities has been abandoned and for the moment money means nothing and cannot be spent. Barter has replaced it.
>
> All shops have either been looted by Communist soldiers for such things as watches and transistor radios, or their goods have been taken away in an organized manner to be stored as communal property.
>
> Even the roads that radiate out of the capital and that carried the nation's commerce have been virtually abandoned. The population living along the roads, as well as that in all cities and towns that remained under the control of the American-backed Government, has been pushed into the interior. Apparently the areas into which the evacuees are being herded are at least 65 miles from Phnom Penh.
>
> In sum, the new rulers — before their overwhelming victory they were known as the Khmer Rouge — appear to be remaking Cambodian society in the peasant image, casting aside everything that belonged to the old system, which was generally dominated by the cities and towns and by the elite and merchants who lived there.
>
> Judging from their present actions, it seems possible that they may largely isolate their country of perhaps seven million people from the rest of the world for a considerable time — at least until the period of upheaval is over, the agrarian revolution takes concrete shape and they are ready to show their accomplishments to foreigners.
>
> Some of the party officials in Phnom Penh also talked about changing the capital to a more traditional and rural town like Siem Reap, in the northwest.
>
> For those foreigners, including this correspondent, who stayed behind to observe the take-over, the events were an astonishing spectacle. ”

Sydney H. Schanberg, *New York Times*, 8 May 1975, quoted in *The Killing Fields: The Facts behind the Film*, Coronet, London, 1984, p. 66

Genocide

The effect of this mass evacuation of the cities, and the relocation of many villages, was to turn Cambodia into one huge labour camp. Evacuees had to find a village that would accept them and, once they were there, they were rarely allowed to leave unless it was at the Khmer Rouge's direction. The 'new' people were usually segregated from the 'old' people, and the new people were usually the last to be fed and the first to die. Villages were controlled by Khmer Rouge cadres, usually men in their 30s, who exercised power through the soldiers. 'The most frightening were the 12- and 13-year-old Khmer Rouge soldiers, because they did not have any humanity, they didn't believe in God, in Buddha, only what the Angka told them to believe.'[2] 'Angka' was the term (meaning Higher Organisation) used to refer to the higher levels of the party. Angka ordered the people to work, usually on large irrigation projects. They were amateur efforts that sometimes assumed that water could run uphill.

> "No civil engineer was involved, for Western science and technology were condemned as bourgeois learning. Trained Kampuchean engineers were Western-educated enemies to be exterminated... Major dams were constructed on the same principles as small ones across minor streams, without the use of theodilites or other instruments and by men with little or no technical training who learned as they went. Practical knowledge learned on the job, through trial and error, was prized above anything to be found in books. Such knowledge was pure and Kampuchean."

Stuart-Fox, *The Murderous Revolution*, p. 132

> "The weird thing about this peasant revolution was that none of the accumulated wisdom of the peasants went into it. When I was a child I hadn't the slightest idea about cultivation. I learnt from Chan and Long on our estate. And I learnt more without trying than after all this effort by the Khmer Rouge. Even when I was a leader I never heard a discussion about agriculture. It was as if the peasants who ruled us despised the fact that they had been peasants. They were choked with power. They had turned their backs on everything they knew for the sake of politics about which they knew nothing. And because they forced us to pretend that we knew nothing, nobody in the society knew anything. If a skilled engineer looking at what they were doing had laid down his spade and offered to design a wonderfully functioning reservoir, he would have been killed for not being a peasant. The whole society was working at maximum — and brutally enforced — inefficiency."

Someth May, *Cambodian Witness*, Faber & Faber, London, 1988, p. 209

The population of Cambodia before the Khmer Rouge was 7 million. The number who died during this brutal three years was between 1 and 2 million. Before Pol Pot, Cambodia produced plenty of food and exported rice. Most of the people during the Pol Pot period died of starvation or diseases related to malnutrition. The death rates varied depending on the area, as those areas where the Khmer Rouge power was most secure tended to have the lowest death rates. There were many reasons for people dying, such as:

- execution for being in Lon Nol's Army, or being a Government official
- being able to read, or having glasses
- having sex (only arranged marriages were allowed)
- stealing food
- because a Khmer Rouge soldier did not like you
- being blown up by a mine while escaping from Kampuchea.

Finally, the Khmer Rouge turned on itself. In the Tuol Sleng prison in Phnom

This map of Cambodia, on display in the Tuol Sleng prison building in Phnom Penh, is made of the skulls of some of the 20 000 Cambodians who were executed in the prison by the Khmer Rouge

Penh, 20 000 people were tortured and executed. All but 1000 of these were Khmer Rouge cadres and their wives and children.

The experiences of Someth May give some idea of the tragedy.[3] Fourteen members of his family left Phnom Penh, and only four survived. His father, a surgeon, was tortured to death. Two cousins were sick from overwork at a dam site, so they were taken to the 'infirmary' where they were mortared. The others died of diseases such as 'swelling sickness' and from dysentery (caused by eating raw paddy crabs).

Research

You can develop a clearer idea of the full impact of the Khmer Rouge on the Cambodian people through personal accounts. The film *The Killing Fields* should be seen. The actor playing Dith Pran in that film, Dr Haing Ngor, claims that his personal experiences were much worse than those of Dith Pran, in that Pran was only tortured once and has been reunited with all his family. If you read Dr Ngor's book, *Surviving the Killing Fields*, you could only agree with him. Other accounts worth reading are the ones mentioned in this chapter, *Cambodian Witness* by Someth May and *The Murderous Revolution* by Martin Stuart-Fox.

THE THIRD INDO-CHINESE WAR

The Vietnamese invasion

The Khmer Rouge period was dominated by terror and paranoia. The regime controlled every aspect of life and used terror to ensure the obedience of all people. Pol Pot seemed to be in a hurry to secure his power against any possible threats, and he perceived the greatest threat would come from the traditional enemy of the Cambodians, the Vietnamese. A rift rapidly developed between the Communist governments of the two countries, based on a number of factors:

- Ideological differences. The Khmer Rouge supported a Maoist form of peasant Communism, whilst the Vietnamese had based their Communist ideas on the centrally controlled Soviet Union style.
- Sino-Soviet rivalry. Vietnam was backed by the Soviets. The Chinese did not trust the Soviets, and were very fearful of being encircled by the Soviets and their allies, the Vietnamese. China gave considerable support to the Khmer Rouge to stop any further increase in Vietnamese power.
- Fear that Vietnam was aiming to bring all of Indo China into an Indo-Chinese Federation, controlled by Vietnam.
- The desire of the Khmer Rouge to revive the glories of the Angkor Empire when southern Vietnam (Kampuchea Krom) was ruled by the Khmers.

During 1977, the Khmer Rouge raced against time to stockpile rice for the war they saw as inevitable. During 1977 and 1978 they staged a series of very brutal attacks across the border into Vietnam, with an estimated 30 000 Vietnamese being killed in these attacks. In December 1977, the Khmer Rouge broke off diplomatic relations with Vietnam. The Vietnamese retaliated with an attack in early 1978 that penetrated thirty kilometres into Cambodia. Khmer Rouge paranoia increased, and they purged all units in the Eastern Provinces of any possible 'Vietnamese contamination'. The Khmer Rouge became consumed by its own internal struggles, with its own members now being the victims.

Relations between Vietnam and China also soured during 1978. The Chinese were undoubtedly aware of the massive purges in Kampuchea, but were committed to supporting the Khmer Rouge in an effort to weaken Vietnam. Most Vietnamese cities had a large population of ethnic Chinese who played an important part in the economic life of the cities. During 1978, the Vietnamese further implemented their Communist policies by banning private trade, a measure that would directly affect the Chinese. Many hundreds of thousands of these Chinese fled Vietnam during 1978.

Following another border attack by the Khmer Rouge, the Vietnamese launched a full-scale invasion of Kampuchea in late December 1978. They attacked directly up the road to Phnom Penh, with the aim of capturing the capital quickly and splitting the Khmer Rouge forces. Phnom Penh fell on 7 January, only a day after Pol Pot and the Khmer Rouge leaders had fled to the jungles of western Kampuchea. Sihanouk was released from house arrest, and left Kampuchea to live in Beijing. On 10 January, the Vietnamese set up a new government in Phnom Penh, under the leadership of Heng Samrin, a former Khmer Rouge leader who had fled to Vietnam in 1978 to escape the purges. The Vietnamese Army then proceeded to move through the rest of Kampuchea, isolating the Khmer Rouge in the jungles near the Thai border.

Discuss

- Why did Vietnam decide to invade Kampuchea? Which of the following reasons is most likely? Give reasons for your choice.
  - (a) The border fighting provided the Vietnamese with an excuse for something that was always going to happen.
  - (b) The Vietnamese wanted to save the Cambodian people from the brutality of the Khmer Rouge.
  - (c) The Vietnamese were acting to protect their own territory from attack.
  - (d) The Vietnamese had plans to expand into Kampuchea, and to then encourage Vietnamese people to move there to settle.
  - (e) The Soviet Union had requested the Vietnamese to attack.
- What might have happened to Kampuchea if Vietnam had not invaded?
- Under what circumstances might one country be justified in invading another country? You might consider recent examples in countries such as Iraq, Nicaragua, the former Yugoslavian states and Somalia.

Chinese attack

The Chinese were quick to respond in defence of the Khmer Rouge. They massed 200 000 troops on the Vietnamese border, and on 18 February launched an attack. The main aims of this attack were:

- To divert Vietnamese troops to the north so that Pol Pot's forces would have a chance to regroup and possibly to launch a counter-attack.
- To boost the morale of other countries in the region, particularly Thailand, which felt threatened by the sudden Vietnamese push.[4]

The attack proved embarrassing for the Chinese, as they suffered heavy casualties. The Vietnamese were able to handle the attack without Soviet support and without affecting their control of Kampuchea.

International reaction

Other countries also reacted against Vietnam's invasion of Kampuchea. These reactions were very important in establishing the pattern of foreign attitudes towards Kampuchea that has persisted since 1979.

United States: The USA still could not come to terms with its defeat at the hands of the Vietnamese, and was opposed to any increase in Vietnamese power.

Thailand: Thailand strongly opposed Vietnamese control of Kampuchea. It saw itself as the dominant economic power in Indo China, and felt that Vietnam could pose a threat to its power.
ASEAN nations: They were concerned that Vietnamese expansion into Kampuchea could increase the role of the Soviet Union in South East Asia, and were worried at the emergence of Vietnam as a strong Communist power, and ally of the Soviet Union.
Australia: Australia felt obliged to go along with the policy of the United States. Aid to Vietnam was stopped.
United Nations: It voted to recognise the Khmer Rouge as the legitimate government of Kampuchea, and the representative of that country at the United Nations.

Review

- Can you explain Australia's vote in the United Nations to recognise the Khmer Rouge as the government of Kampuchea?
- What other action could Australia have taken at the time?

Famine and refugees

The removal of the Khmer Rouge did not immediately improve the lives of the people. The year 1979 was one of severe famine, with up to half the population of some villages dying. The organisational structure in many villages collapsed, and irrigation was abandoned. The people took to the roads to try and find their families and their homes. At least 600 000 Cambodians headed for the Thai border, and camps were set up along both sides of it.

The Vietnamese were at first reluctant to admit the extent of the famine, and it was not until mid-1979 that other countries became aware of the devastation caused by the Khmer Rouge, and of the famine. UNICEF and the Red Cross led the international effort to feed Cambodia, and over $500 million was provided in the next two years. There was a reluctance to send this aid directly to Phnom Penh, where it was controlled by the Vietnamese. At first, up to half the aid was sent to the border camps where a huge smuggling operation was started to get the food into Cambodia. The smugglers were paid inside Cambodia with gold that had been hidden during the Khmer Rouge years. Smuggling became a way of life for many of the camp people, and became the major economic activity inside Cambodia.[5]

Many of the camps were controlled by black marketeers and warlords. Others were controlled directly by the Khmer Rouge who used the camps as a base to continue the fight against Heng Samrin's Government. All of the camps were fed by the relief agencies so that the United Nations, in effect, gave

Amputees in a clinic in Battambang, Cambodia, being trained to use their artificial legs (courtesy Rob Elliott)

direct support to the Khmer Rouge. The Chinese supplied the Khmer Rouge with arms, and the Thais allowed this process to continue without interference. There were many attacks on the camps up to 1985 by the Vietnamese and the Thais, and by those in rival camps. In early 1992, when the United Nations began the process of moving them back to Cambodia, 370 000 Cambodians still lived in the camps.

The Vietnamese occupation

The Vietnamese were welcomed at first by the Cambodians as their saviours from the genocidal Khmer Rouge. However, the longer the Vietnamese stayed the more they could be portrayed as invaders, and the Heng Samrin Government depicted as their puppets. Propaganda broadcasts from sources such as the United States promoted this view, as did the diplomatic isolation imposed on Cambodia. The United Nations denied Cambodia any access to development aid, and refused to recognise Heng Samrin's Government.

Vietnamese officials took over positions throughout Cambodia, as there were few educated Cambodians who had survived the Khmer Rouge. Many Vietnamese people moved into Cambodia to settle, evoking traditional fears of Vietnamese expansion. For 700 years, the Vietnamese had used the migration of their people into other areas to extend their country's borders and it seemed the same thing was now happening in Cambodia. The obvious presence in

Cambodia of 200 000 Vietnamese soldiers added to the fears of the Cambodians, and the Vietnamese were increasingly seen as invaders rather than saviours.

Gary Klintworth disagrees with the view of the Vietnamese as invaders:

> "The Vietnamese army has had a good 'hearts and minds' relationship with the local Cambodians for two reasons. First, they were on the whole strictly disciplined and well behaved; there were few reports of assaults or stealing by Vietnamese soldiers. Secondly, the Vietnamese intervention in Cambodia was regarded as an act of liberation by the majority of Cambodians...
>
> In evaluating the Vietnamese intervention in Cambodia, we might ask the question — have the Cambodians suffered under the Vietnamese in the last ten years? The answer must be no. The Vietnamese presence in Cambodia has not been the oppressive army of occupation that it is often made out to be. It has, on the contrary, been a model of good behaviour. It has helped to reconstruct a society and an economy that was for all practical purposes almost completely destroyed by the Khmer Rouge."

Gary Klintworth, 'Vietnam in Cambodia', *Current Affairs Bulletin*, September 1989, pp. 26–7

The Tripartite Coalition

Resistance to the Vietnamese developed in the camps along the Thai border, with three distinct groups emerging:

Khmer Rouge: The Party of Democratic Kampuchea. After 1985, Khieu Samphan became official leader, but Pol Pot was still in charge.

Sihanoukists: Officially the FUNCINPEC (the National United Front for an Independent, Neutral, Peaceful and Cooperative Cambodia).

KPNLF: Khmer People's National Liberation Armed Forces. The KPNLF was formed in 1979 by former Prime Minister Son Sann from the free Khmer who had settled in the camps.

In June 1982, the members of ASEAN helped to get the three groups to co-operate against the Vietnamese. A loose coalition was formed, called the Coalition Government of Democratic Kampuchea (CGDK) with Prince Sihanouk as President and Chief of State, Son Sann as Prime Minister and head of government, and Khieu Samphan as Vice President of Foreign Affairs. The three groups continued to control their own camps and resistance armies, but the United Nations was able to allow the CGDK to occupy Cambodia's seat at the UN. The CGDK changed its name to the National Government of Cambodia (NGC) in 1990.

Review

- List the reasons why the Cambodian people would come to resent the Vietnamese occupation. Would the attitude of the peasants be the same as the attitude of the people in Phnom Penh?
- What evidence is there to support Klintworth's favourable view of the occupation?
- Why would ASEAN nations encourage the formation of the Tripartite Coalition?
- What right did this coalition have to claim Cambodia's seat at the United Nations?

The empty faces of these women at a market in Phnom Penh in 1992 reflect the effects of the past on their lives and their concern for the future (courtesy Rob Elliott)

Vietnamese withdrawal

In 1979, Vietnam had 225 000 soldiers in Cambodia, but this number gradually declined during the 1980s, until only 100 000 were left by 1988. Vietnam's withdrawal then accelerated, until the last Vietnamese troops were withdrawn in September 1989. There were many complex reasons for Vietnam's withdrawal, with the domestic situation in Vietnam being the most important. Some of these reasons were:

Vietnamese economy: Vietnam had an inflation rate of about 500 per cent, 30 per cent unemployment, and declining rice production, but was trying to maintain the third largest army in the world (at 1.2 million).

Perestroika: Gorbachev was pursuing reforms in the Soviet Union that were leading to the end of the Cold War and better relations with China, which he visited in May 1989. Internal reforms in the Soviet Union also meant that the Soviets could no longer afford to subsidise Vietnam's war in Cambodia.

United States: The US had told Vietnam that it would start diplomatic relations after its withdrawal. Vietnam was increasingly suffering from its diplomatic isolation from the US, and particularly wanted the trade and financial aid that would follow its ending.

Cambodia: Klintworth points out that 'Vietnam could not completely trust the government of Heng Samrin — it was Cambodian first and foremost'.[6]

Khmer Rouge: The Vietnamese felt that the Khmer Rouge were no longer strong enough to take over Cambodia, particularly if an agreement between the Soviets and the Chinese led to their withdrawal of support for them. Sihanouk also seemed to be changing his position. '"Hun Sen (now Cambodian Prime Minister) was", said Prince Sihanouk, "80 per cent good and only 20 per cent bad... he is my son, a bad boy but not so bad!!!"'[7]

Casualties: 55 000 Vietnamese died in Cambodia, and 60 000 were wounded. Many more suffered from diseases such as malaria.

The United Nations Agreement

The visit of President Gorbachev of the Soviet Union to China in May 1989 was an event that clearly symbolised the changing world, and indicated the impact these changes would have on Indo China. Vietnam now could not be backed up by the crumbling Soviet Union, and it was more important that it rebuild its relations with China. China also started to look towards building contacts with Vietnam. These changes meant that Cambodia was no longer important in the struggle between the Super Powers and, because it had no real strategic or economic value, the major powers — China, the Soviet Union and the United States — lost interest in Cambodia. Other groups, such as ASEAN and the United Nations, became actively involved in the search for a Cambodian settlement.

The impending withdrawal of Vietnamese troops from Cambodia accelerated moves to set up a democratically elected government. The four main parties in Cambodia met in Paris in August 1989. Prince Sihanouk and Hun Sen were able to shake hands during the Conference, but the attitude of the Khmer Rouge stopped any agreement. This failure led to a resumption of the war, with the coalition groups (the Khmer Rouge and the supporters of Sihanouk and Son Sann) attacking the Hun Sen Government.

> "It was in that context that Senator Evans (Australian Minister of Foreign Affairs) launched an initiative which, at the time, was seen as but a modest suggestion or policy adjustment.
>
> The fundamental idea was simple... an impartial general election, organised by the United Nations and internationally supervised...
>
> Senator Evans suggested that the UN be involved in the administration of Cambodia during the transitional period, subject to an appropriate change in the status of the Cambodian seat at the UN."

R. Sturkey, 'Cambodia: Issues for Negotiation in a Comprehensive Settlement', in *Backgrounder*, vol. 18/1, 29 June 1990

Senator Evans' plan was proposed in November 1989, and was actively promoted around the world by Evans and his senior diplomat, Michael Costello. In January, they gained acceptance for the proposal from the permanent members of the UN Security Council — China, France, Britain, the USA and the Soviet Union. A series of very difficult meetings between the four Cambodian parties then followed, resulting in the four agreeing in October to a settlement. The main features of this agreement were:

- Demobilisation of 70 per cent of the forces of each group, under UN supervision.
- Repatriation of 350 000 refugees from camps in Thailand.
- Recognition of the Supreme National Council (SNC) as the interim government, made up of 12 representatives from the four Cambodian factions.
- Return of Sihanouk as Head of State, and leader of the SNC.
- Creation of UNTAC (UN Transitional Authority in Cambodia) to supervise the peace process — particularly demobilisation, repatriation and the elections planned for May 1993.
- Creation of a peace-keeping force.

The Peace Agreement made no mention of the genocidal policies of the Khmer Rouge, as they had consistently refused to sign any treaty that mentioned their atrocities. In fact, the treaty could be seen to be have given official recognition to the Khmer Rouge.

OBSTACLES TO PEACE

Japan's Yakushi Akashi was appointed the head of UNTAC, and Major-General John Sanderson of Australia, the Military Commander. These appointments showed the importance of the roles of Australia and Japan in Cambodia, with Japan sending troops overseas for the first time since 1945. UNTAC had an estimated budget of $2 billion, 15 900 troops and about 6000 police and bureaucrats by early 1993.

During 1992, UNTAC gradually began implementing the changes in Cambodia. The main problems it experienced were:

- Refusal of the Khmer Rouge to disarm.
- Khmer Rouge claims that Vietnamese troops remain in Cambodia.
- The barring of UN troops, by the Khmer Rouge, from areas it controls.
- Increasing corruption in the cities creating a situation that the Khmer Rouge could exploit.

Review

- List the main stages of the peace process.
- Why have Australia and Japan played such an important role in Cambodia?
- What did the Khmer Rouge gain from the Peace Agreement? Did it make any concessions?
- Examine recent events in Cambodia to determine the extent to which the Peace Agreement of October 1991 has been carried out.

Indecent peace process leaves mass murderers holding the whip hand

By TIZIANO TERZANI
of Der Spiegal

ON a Bangkok-Phnom Penh flight not long ago, I found myself sitting next to a mass murderer. Had he been a member of Hitler's Nazi Party, he would have been a hunted man — but he was a Cambodian, a member of the Khmer Rouge.

As such he enjoys the protection of the United Nations and, in the diplomatic circles he frequents, is called deferentially "His Excellency Khieu Samphan".

The indecency of the whole UN peace plan for Cambodia shows up in the fact that an innocent traveller can nowadays find himself in such company. Three weeks ago, I saw the chief of the UN Transitional Authority in Cambodia, Yasushi Akashi, blocked by a bamboo pole across a dirt road a few metres from the centre of the "Khmer Rouge capital" of Pailin.

Two communist guerillas stood guard with their AK-47 rifles while a third rode off on a bicycle to see whether his political commissar would allow the UN convoy to proceed. He did not return.

An indecent episode if one considers that those young soldiers were taking orders from the cadres responsible for one of the worst crimes committed this century: the Cambodian holocaust.

Since the signing of the Paris agreement in October, the Khmer Rouge — alone among the four warring Cambodian factions — has profited from the new situation. It has gained political legitimacy inside and outside Cambodia while expanding the area under its control.

Having discovered that no one is ready to call its bluff, the Khmer Rouge has constantly raised the stakes — and won every time. In return, UNTAC has increased the number of observation posts along the Vietnamese border to prove its "goodwill" to the Khmer Rouge.

The Khmer Rouge has managed to get away with all manner of breaches of the Paris agreement.

Two months ago, the secretary-general of the UN, Dr Boutros Boutros Ghali, visited Cambodia to throw his weight behind the UN peace operation. In a formal speech, referring to the years when the Khmer Rouge was in power and killed or let die possibly one-third of the Cambodian population, he spoke of "grave mistakes of the past".

During his three-day stay in Cambodia, Boutros Ghali managed to visit various places — including a minefield where he attended probably the first and last UN demining operation. He did not, however, visit the Tuol Sleng museum — Phnom Penh's Auschwitz — nor pay respect to the monument dedicated to the victims of the Cambodian holocaust. An indecent omission.

The indecency continues, UNTAC has so far brought some 13,000 people to Cambodia. Most are not there to help Cambodia but to pursue their personal or national interests. Even junior officers in the UNTAC peacekeeping force earn around $US60,000 ($81,000) a year.

Germany has used Cambodia as the occasion for sending soldiers outside the NATO area for the first time since World War II. Japan may do the same. Indonesia has sent two battalions so as to be forgiven for the massacre committed by its forces in East Timor, while the Thais, having exploited every aspect of the war, are now trying to exploit the peace and have sent soldiers to establish the basis for their economic control of western Cambodia.

The *Weekend Australian*, 4–5 July, 1992, p. 24

Structured questions

- Why did Prince Sihanouk fail to keep Cambodia out of the conflict that developed in Vietnam?
- Why was the Khmer Rouge able to defeat the Lon Nol Government?
- What have been the effects on Cambodia of the Khmer Rouge from 1975 up until the present?

Review

Complete the following table. What do the symbols and the colours represent? The three white stars represent the Cambodian people and the 'captive' Khmer in Thailand and Vietnam.

Blue White Yellow Red

	Official name of the country	*Type of government*	*Main features of the period*
Sihanouk 1955–1970 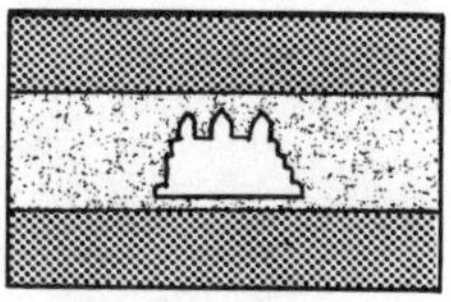			
Lon Nol 1970–1975 			
Pol Pot 1976–1979 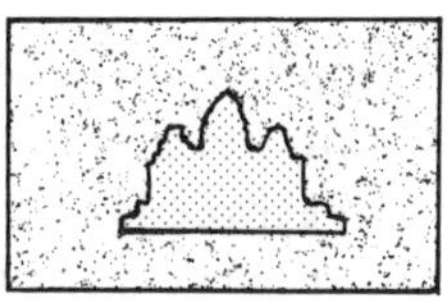			
Hun Sen 1979–1991 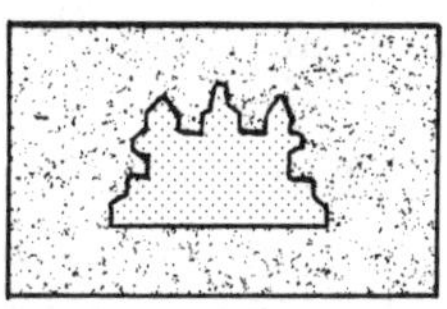			
1991–1992 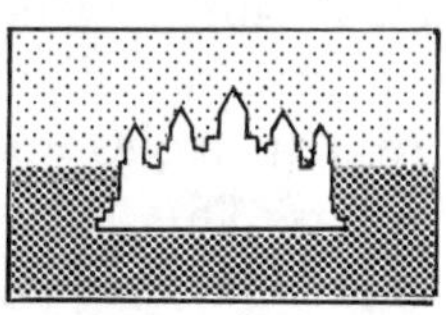			
1993– 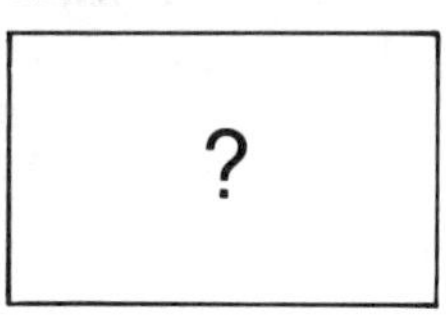			

Adapted from the *Sydney Morning Herald*, 3 May, 1989

LAOS

CHAPTER THIRTEEN

HISTORICAL BACKGROUND

LAOS is a very mountainous and under-populated country that has suffered through history from being trapped in the middle of strong neighbours: Vietnam, Thailand and China. The largest of the four main ethnic groups are the Lao people, who moved into Laos from southern China probably during the eighth century BC. They now make up half the population, with the original tribal inhabitants, the Lao Theung, comprising another 15 per cent. Tribal Thai groups and the Hmong, originally from China, each make up about another 15 per cent.

The earlier kingdoms of Laos were first united in 1353 by King Fa Ngum, who had been brought up by the Khmers at Angkor. He brought with him a Khmer wife, and set up Buddhism as the state religion. Fa Ngum united Lan Xang (Laos) and organised its administration, as well as extending its borders to include parts of Thailand. His successors further extended Laos, and developed a religious lifestyle with the *wat* (temple) as the centre of village life. Lan Xang declined in the 16th century following internal struggles and conflicts with Burma, Siam (Thailand), Vietnam and the Khmers. This led to the division of Laos in 1694 into three principalities, and to a gradual increase in Siamese influence. The Siamese invaded Laos in 1778, sacked the capital of Vientiane and took the Emerald Buddha statue back to Bangkok where it still remains. The Lao kings of the three kingdoms remained, but were under Siamese control.

French influence

During the 19th century, the French extended their influence throughout Indo China, including Laos where Siamese influence was gradually replaced by the French. The French re-united the many small kingdoms into the Kingdom of Laos. In 1899 the kingdom was officially declared a Protectorate of France, and Laos became one of the five parts of French Indo China. A treaty in 1907 with Thailand set out the present borders.

Japanese occupation

The Japanese occupied Laos during World War II. At the end of their occupation, the Japanese encouraged the Prime Minister to declare Laos an independent monarchy, and King Sisavang Vong was crowned as king. In September 1945 the Lao Issara (Free Lao), an anti-French nationalist movement, overthrew the King. The following April, the Lao Issara combined with the monarchists to establish a constitutional monarchy. However, the French returned to Laos in late 1946. They allowed token independence for Laos, accepted a new constitution in 1947, and gave Laos formal independence within the French Union in 1949.

GROWTH OF NATIONALIST RESISTANCE MOVEMENTS

There was still considerable nationalist resistance to the French, which developed in two directions: the Lao Issara (Free Lao) and the Pathet Lao (the Lao Communists). The Pathet Lao gained control of much of northern Laos, where it established an alternative administration and carried out a program of social and economic reform. It also worked closely with the Viet Minh, who were fighting against the French in nearby northern Vietnam. An attempt by the Viet Minh to spread the war into Laos caused the French to try and thwart this by fortifying Dien Bien Phu. This lead to the eventual defeat of the French. The Geneva Conference which ended the French War in 1954 granted full independence to Laos, and set up a coalition government which included the Pathet Lao along with the monarchists and Lao Issara representatives. The King remained as head of state. Prince Souvanna Phouma was the neutralist Prime Minister, and Prince Souphanouvong leader of the increasingly Communist Pathet Lao.

Review

- Compare the experiences of Laos and Vietnam under French rule.
- How did Laos avoid war in its anti-French struggle?

A memorial arch in central Vientiane shows clearly the mixture of cultural influences on Laos, from French to Indian (courtesy Mark Hall)

COLLAPSE OF THE COALITION GOVERNMENT

The Coalition Government was always fragile, and it started to split after the Pathet Lao won over half the seats at the 1958 elections. In 1959, Souphanouvong and other Pathet Lao leaders were arrested, leading to an increase in armed resistance from the northern provinces. Attempts over the next three years to re-establish a coalition government all failed, and Laos became increasingly split. For the next twelve years it was effectively divided into two warring states, with the Royal Lao army controlling the few cities along the Mekong, and the Pathet Lao holding most of the countryside.

INVOLVEMENT IN THE VIETNAM WAR

The official Lao Government, based in Vientiane, became more conservative and gained the support of the United States who sent military advisers and supplies. Meanwhile the Pathet Lao were heavily backed by North Vietnam.

As the war between North and South Vietnam developed, Laos became directly involved. From 1963, North Vietnam began to use the Ho Chi Minh trail through Laos, and North Vietnam kept many troops in the area. The Americans increased their military support for the Royal Lao Government, and began heavy bombing attacks on the trail, using fake markings to cover their involvement. US involvement was carried out through the CIA, and the war in Laos was directed from the US embassy in Vientiane. The United States also gained support from the Hmong tribesmen in their struggle against the Pathet Lao. The result of US involvement was similar to the effects of the secret bombing of Cambodia. The massive bombing failed to cut the Ho Chi Minh Trail and defeat the Pathet Lao, but it did turn over 10 per cent of the people into refugees and, in the process, increased support for the Pathet Lao.

The winding down of the war in Vietnam meant that the military struggle in Laos turned into a political one. Direct fighting stopped in early 1973 and a coalition government was formed which included Communist representation. The Communists used this coalition to increase their support throughout Laos, and their position was greatly strengthened by Communist victories in Cambodia and Vietnam in 1975. Many supporters of the old government fled Laos when they saw the Communists taking over in Phnom Penh and Saigon. Vietnamese Communists were closely involved in the increasing power of the Pathet Lao. On 28 November the Provisional Government collapsed under Communist pressure, and on 2 December the King abdicated and the monarchy was abolished. The Lao People's Democratic Republic was established by the Communist Pathet Lao, with Prince Souphanouvong President. The last two years of their thirty-year struggle had been relatively non-violent.

Review

Maclear quotes the US Ambassador in Laos from 1964 to 1968 as saying:

> “Laos wasn't the center of activity, and since we didn't wish to get the United States forces directly involved in a confrontation there while the confrontation was being pursued in South Vietnam, it was decided not to take an overt cognizance of this breakdown (of neutrality), and to continue to operate in a covert way.”

Maclear, *Vietnam: The Ten Thousand Day War*, p. 242

- Why does the Ambassador say that the US wanted the war to be 'covert'?
- What measures did the US take to carry on this covert war?
- How important to the United States was Laos?

THE PHONGSAVAN FAMILY

My husband had been an official in the Royal Lao Government and we had lived a comfortable life in Vientiane up to 1975, largely untouched by the civil war. After the Pathet Lao took over, we began to hear of concentration camps that had been set up in northern Laos. Like most Government officials, my husband was sent off to the camps, but they let him come back after only a month. Very few people ever came back. All the Laotian people were very upset when the King and his family were sent to the camps. When my husband came back, he had to work very hard for the communist government as a charcoal burner, leaving for the jungle about midnight and returning late in the day. He did not get any money from the charcoal, but was given a very small monthly salary by the government. The people who had been well paid before were given the lowest salaries, and the people who had been the poorest paid were given higher salaries. The new government sent all of the people from the city to help during the rice season, and my eight year old girl had to plant rice. In Vientiane, we had to meet three mornings a week for sessions that would last about half an hour. We were told how corrupt the old government was, but we knew that it was hard to get food and that we had lost our freedom. The new communist government people had plenty to eat and lived in big houses with electrified fences. These people had been to Moscow to study, and when they came back they looked pleasant, but inside they were very bad.

In the city, we knew that there was a camp on an island about 80 km from Vientiane. At first, about 300 people were sent there; business people and playboys. More and more people were sent, but nobody came back. In 1978, we were told that our family would be sent to the camp in two days, so we decided to leave. We left the city after midnight and went to a place in the jungle we had been told about. I had to carry my youngest child. Some Laotians took us across the Mekong River in a small boat, and we were met by some Thais. We paid them 2000 baht (about $100) for each person. Our family stayed in a refugee camp in Thailand for 18 months before we were accepted to come to Australia. My eldest daughter was now 12, and her education had been very interrupted. We could not afford English lessons in the camp. When we came to Australia, she started school in Wollongong and she has now completed an Honours degree at University.

From an interview with the author

The wedding of Thonglenane and Amphone Phongsavan in Vientiane in 1965. This wedding photo was one of the few possessions the Phongsavans could take with them when they fled from Laos in 1978 (courtesy the Phongsavan family)

LAOS UNDER COMMUNISM

The new government had been able to take power with the backing of the Vietnamese, and the form of Communism introduced also followed the Vietnamese example:

- The media was closely controlled.
- The social system was changed to weaken the middle class and support the peasants.
- Central economic planning was introduced, replacing private ownership with state-owned enterprises and communes.
- Internal and external trade became difficult.
- Many thousands of supporters of the old government were arrested and put into re-education camps.

Over 30 000 Vietnamese troops remained in Laos, and Vietnamese influence on the government was strong. This was largely because the Laotians and Vietnamese had co-operated closely in the past, and because both were isolated diplomatically and feared the Chinese. The strong presence of the Vietnamese was seen by some as part of an attempt by them to dominate Indo China.

Laos also suffered the same problems and failures as did Vietnam. Hundreds of thousands of Laotians — 325 000 in fact — fled to Thailand, many of them from the Hmong people who had fought for the Americans. In 1987, 120 000 of these people still lived in refugee camps in Thailand. Economically, Communism in Laos failed, and the people increasingly struggled to survive. From 1985, under the label of New Economic Mechanism (NEM), the Communist government began to slowly change the economy to allow more private enterprise. Free market prices replaced prices set by the government. Farmers were allowed to own land and sell crops at market prices. These changes have helped to boost exports, but the whole economy is affected by the backwardness of

Construction of the bridge across the Mekong River, to join Laos and Thailand. This will be the first bridge to cross the Mekong outside China. The Australian government is financing this major project, and it is being constructed by the Australian company, John Holland (courtesy John Holland)

agriculture. Since 1989, attempts to stimulate the economy have increased, including a freer approach to foreign investment, and the privatisation of public firms. The government has also tried hard to attract foreign investment.

Changes in international relations

Economic changes have been accompanied by a changed attitude to other countries. Laos has looked to increase its ties with Thailand, and decrease its dependence on Vietnam. It has opened its borders so that travel, at least to Vientiane, has become easier. The Mekong River Bridge, currently being built by the Australians near Vientiane, will be vital to this process as it will greatly encourage trade with Thailand and allow Laotian goods to be transported easily to Bangkok.

Laos today

The old-guard leaders of Laos finally granted the people a constitution in August 1991. Kaysone Phomvihane, 71, who had led Laos since 1975, was appointed president. Power was retained by the Soviet-style Communist leaders, and the people will see little change until the old Communists retire. Thirty-three political prisoners have been imprisoned for 15 years without trial, and the media is strictly censored. Laos continues to be one of the world's ten least developed countries, with its economy only surviving through foreign aid. Average life expectancy is only 46 years, and education, communication and transport are severely limited. Travel by road between the two main cities, Vientiane and Luang Prabang, a distance of 200 kilometres, can take two days.

Review

- What have been the main stages in relations between Laos and Vietnam since 1945?
- How did life for the Laotian people change when the Communists took power in 1975?
- Why did so many people flee from Laos between 1975 and 1980? What groups of people would have had the strongest reasons for leaving?

Research

- Why is Laos one of the world's ten least developed countries? Is this situation likely to change?
- What changes have there been in the government of Laos since the death in late 1992 of Kaysone Phomvihane?

INDO CHINA TODAY

CHAPTER FOURTEEN

VIETNAM

Political structure

VIETNAM clearly no longer runs along Communist lines economically, but politically the Communist Party is firmly in control. The main unifying ideology that it has left is the memory of Ho Chi Minh, and this is promoted very strongly by the Party. His portrait is displayed everywhere, and there are Ho Chi Minh Museums in every major city. The people seem able to ignore this, and Ho does not appear to be held in genuine awe by the people. There is considerable resentment in Saigon that the city was forced to officially change its name to Ho Chi Minh City.

Without Ho as a unifying factor, there appears to be little to hold Vietnam together. This lack of a unifying principle will become more important as the gap between North and South widens, as in many ways they are different countries. In 1975, large numbers of Communist officials were sent from Hanoi to take over all the top jobs in the South, and the old business and political leaders either left or were sent to re-education camps. The ordinary people in the South still talk of 1975 as the year 'when the Communists came'. As the North tries to hold on to political control in the South, and to keep some semblance of socialism, resentment is likely to develop. Successful South Vietnamese businessmen, with foreign financial support, will tire of Northern political interference.

In July 1992, supposedly free elections were held for the National Assembly. Non-Communists were allowed to stand, but they had to prove that they were loyal Vietnamese citizens, and the easiest way to prove this was to have belonged to the Communist Party — a catch 22 situation. Candidates were screened, and only two non-Communists were allowed to stand. Many of the Independents who tried to stand were said to have not filled in their applications properly, or were found to have 'health' problems.

The election results did see some changes, with a decline in the number of old-guard Communists, and a greater number of tertiary-educated members. In Hanoi, 14 of the 20 people elected have university degrees. However, real power still remains with the Communist elite in Hanoi.

Economy and society

Decline of Communism

Although as an economic system Communism barely exists any more in Vietnam, the country is still struggling to create an effective economic system to replace it. From 1975 to 1989, the economy was heavily tied to Vietnam's only friend at that time, the Soviet Union. Much money and effort was expended on grandiose Soviet-style projects that did little to help the Vietnamese people, such as:

- The Hoa Binh Hydro-Electric Scheme, designed to supply Vietnam's power needs. (Apart from being an environmental disaster, it is still only working at half capacity because the generation and distribution systems have not been completed.)
- The three-kilometre Thang Long Bridge near Hanoi, designed to be part of a super-highway but which has only dirt roads leading off each end.
- Hanoi's Cultural Centre and Ho's Mausoleum.

The economy followed Soviet-style central planning, with agriculture organised into farming collectives, and factories and businesses owned by the Communist Party Committee in each province. This policy failed and, coupled with the difficulties of post-war recovery and the country's involvement in Cambodia, has left Vietnam a very poor country. The United States' policy of isolating Vietnam has added to its problems as it has meant that official outside aid has been denied it.

Vital Statistics 1992

	Vietnam	*Cambodia*	*(Australia)*
GNP per capita	$200 US	$150 US	($16180 US)
GNP growth	3.8 %	5.0 %	(1.6 %)
Inflation	78.9 %	150 %	(1.2 %)
Exports	$1.9 bn	$0.04 bn	($41.9 bn)
Population	70 m	8.6 m	(17.2 m)
Infant mortality	43/1000	116/1000	(8/1000)
People per telephone	537	790	(1.8)
People per doctor	3.040	27000	(438)

Figures compiled from *Asiaweek*, 23 October, 1992, pp. 12,14

Vietnam made the first move away from Soviet-style Communism in 1986 when it adopted the *Doi Moi* or 'Renovation' policy. Implementation of this policy was accelerated after the 1990 Party Congress and changes since then in Vietnam have been quite significant. Renovation has been designed to move

Workers at Ninh Thien farming collective, near Hanoi, use a typical Vietnamese method to move the rice. How important were bicycles to the Viet Cong during the war?

away from centralised style Communism towards what the Chinese leaders now call Free Market Socialism. The changes are similar to those in Russia in the 1920s under the New Economic Policy.

Changes on a collective

Ninh Thien is a farming village of about 10 000 people near Hanoi. It is one of the more prosperous ex-collectives. The Communist Party officials still control the village and make the major decisions, but the farmers can produce what they want and sell it on the open market. Land has been allocated to the farmers on the basis of their needs and their ability as farmers, and that land is kept by them for 15 years. The Party Committee says that it is encouraging people in the village to specialise in activities that they are good at. Those good at building are encouraged to build houses rather than farm. They are hired by individuals to build houses, and paid in a negotiated manner, usually a mixture of money and goods. Taxes are set by the Party Committee as a percentage of the crops produced or services provided. The Committee has also become actively capitalist, buying goods in China and re-selling them in different parts of Vietnam. The village has a primary school for over 2000 students. Students attend either the morning or the afternoon shift, and are in classes of over 50. The government pays the salary of each teacher, about $14 per month, and the village is responsible for the buildings. There is no high school in the village.

Discuss

- In what ways would this village have changed since the start of the Renovation Policy in 1986?

Industry

The older state-run factories are declining and the number of private factories is increasing rapidly, particularly in the South. Many of the large enterprises are joint ventures between Vietnamese and overseas business people, particularly from Japan, Taiwan, Hong Kong, Singapore, France, Thailand and Australia. The foreigners provide the money, and the Vietnamese try and keep some control by making sure they are closely involved. Many businesses have found it difficult to get going in Vietnam because of the bureaucracy and inconsistent government policy, though quite often well directed 'gifts' can speed up the process. Most industries have developed in areas which can benefit from Vietnam's very cheap labour (workers earn about $20 a month), such as textiles, carpets and food production.

Most goods are sold in street markets, though there is an increasing number of privately owned shops selling a much wider range of consumer goods than in 1990. Hotels are either owned by the Party Committee, or are joint ventures with foreign companies, who provide the finance.

Hard currency

Having been abandoned by the Soviet Union, the Vietnamese leaders would now prefer to follow the Chinese path of Free Market Socialism, but the people want United-States-style capitalism and are desperate for every dollar they can get. Foreigners are separated quite efficiently from their US dollars, and pay four times more for hotels, trains and planes than do the Vietnamese. They are seen as fair game in a country desperate for foreign currency. US dollars are accepted everywhere, even for restaurant meals. The departure tax at the airport can only be paid in US dollars.

One of the main reasons for this desire for foreign currency is that the Vietnamese currency, the *dong*, has been largely wiped out by inflation. One hundred US dollars brings over 1 million dong, usually in 2000- or 5000-dong notes. The banking system in Vietnam is only just starting to develop. Cheques are not used and credit cards have only been heard of in Saigon. Motor bikes and cars are bought with cardboard boxes full of dong.

Renovation

The real renovation of the Vietnamese economy is coming about through individual enterprise, not through government policy. Houses are being rebuilt in the major cities at a rapid rate, as families decide it is now safe to build.

These people may have hoarded the money for years, been given it by overseas relatives, or made money from their business. Some may have made a lot of money from smuggling, as this is a major economic activity and one that the government has little control over. The same frantic building effort is going into building new shops, hotels and offices. The old 'Hanoi Hilton' prison is to be demolished and replaced by a 22-storey office/hotel complex for a Singaporean joint-venture company. This will be the first major non-government building erected in Hanoi since before 1940, and the only one over four storeys.

Renovation in Ho Chi Minh City (Saigon) is much more business oriented, and foreign investors are more active. Shops in Saigon sell mobile phones and computers, devices that are almost non-existent in Hanoi. Major office buildings were built in Saigon in 1992 and more are under construction.

Problems facing Renovation

- **Infrastructure:** The road system is very poor, trains average 30 kilometres per hour, planes are old Russian ones and ports are not developed for containers. An effort is being made to upgrade airports.
- **Education:** Class numbers in high schools are between 50 and 60, and the schools lack any facilities. Teachers are paid less than factory workers, although they maintain a high status in society. The curriculum is still ideologically controlled and lacks substance.
- **Leadership:** The Communist Party is clearly going to remain in power, but the ideological basis of its power has been lost. Its leaders are largely

'Renovation' at work in Hanoi as some of the new rich put their wealth into this house

the men who have presided over the mistakes of Vietnam since 1975.

- **Disunity:** North-South resentment. Political control still comes from the North, but economic growth is generated in the South.
- **Foreign investment:** Many foreign businesses will rush to exploit the situation in Vietnam, with little concern for helping the country.

CAMBODIA

Cambodia is a society that is changing rapidly, but the general direction of that change is difficult to predict because of the many forces at work.

UNTAC (The United Nations' Transitional Authority, Cambodia): There are currently 20 000 UN personnel in Cambodia, each of them with an allowance of over $140 per day in a country where $30 per month was a good salary. Lindsay Murdoch sees Phnom Penh turning from a 'princess' into a seedy UN boom town.

> "Everybody seems to be on the make in Cambodia these days. In a get-rich-quick frenzy, Cambodians who endured two decades of poverty, foreign invasion and war, have sold or are selling everything from real estate to timber to banking concessions... While some UN soldiers are deployed in malaria-infested and heavily mined jungle, a Thai contingent has set up a superb restaurant in Battambang, with fresh supplies trucked across the border."

Lindsay Murdoch, 'Once a princess, Cambodia's capital now a seedy UN boom town', *Sydney Morning Herald*, 31 August, 1992, p. 12

This invasion has greatly accelerated the corruption in Phnom Penh, led to severe inflation, doubled the number of brothels, and pushed up the price of housing past levels the Cambodians can afford. At some stage, the UN will leave, and the effects of this withdrawal could be just as drastic on the lives of the people as the invasion.

Resettlement: Over 300 000 refugees are being brought back from camps along the Thai border for resettlement. There are huge problems in this process, made more acute by Khmer Rouge control of large areas of Cambodia.

Government: Elections are to be held in May 1993. Will they result in a stable government for Cambodia? What will be the attitude of the Khmer Rouge?

Demobilisation: As part of the UN peace process, soldiers from the four factions are supposed to hand in their arms, although the Khmer Rouge are refusing. Many soldiers from the other factions have turned to banditry as a way of life.

Racism: Racial hatred between Khmers and Viets goes back two hundred years, to when the Vietnamese moved into, and took over, the Mekong Delta area from the Khmers. Return of this land has been an important element in Khmer attitudes since then. There are significant areas within the delta of Khmer people. Many Vietnamese have moved into Cambodia in the past few years, and there are possibly one million there at present. This has provoked Cambodian resentment, and given the Khmer Rouge one major issue which it can exploit. A Western diplomat, quoted by Lindsay Murdoch, said:

> "The presence of Vietnamese inside Cambodia is the absolute central cause of this country's problems. The 100 percent feeling of Cambodians, even those who supported Vietnam's invasion to oust Pol Pot, is that there are too many Vietnamese in the country. The Vietnamese badly mistreated Cambodians during the years they occupied the country. If you ask ordinary Cambodians whether they would prefer domination by the Khmer Rouge or Vietnamese, they will say the Khmer Rouge."

Sydney Morning Herald, 24 August, 1992, p. 11

Effects of war

Behind the headlines Cambodia rots away

As the world frets about growing political violence in Cambodia, it fails to notice a society turning the gun on itself. LOUISE WILLIAMS reports.

IN BROAD daylight on the crowded main street of Phnom Penh a police jeep recently knocked a cyclist off his bike. The policeman stopped and went over to where the man lay injured. The driver pulled out his gun and shot the man dead like a downed horse.

The hundreds of people who witnessed the murder did not attempt to protest or intervene, according to an Australian official, who was one car back in the traffic. The crowd's apparent indifference, he said, was even more disturbing than the killing.

Violence with a political label usually dominates our thinking on Cambodia. But, in reality it is violence without a political label that rules the lives of ordinary Cambodians. It is now common, not extraordinary, for armed gangs in Phnom Penh to kill for a motor-bike. The motor bikes are valuable resale items for the markets in Vietnam or even southern China.

It is also common for soldiers or policemen, or anyone else with a gun, to establish "freelance" road blocks around the country at night and to extort petty fees in exchange for safe passage. It is common, not extraordinary, for families to assault their relatives in disputes over household occupancy and for men to assault their wives in disputes over virtually anything at all.

"The average Cambodian thinks that the only way to solve a dispute is through deceit and violence, even if proper legal channels exist," said Lyndall Maclean, who has worked in Cambodia for the United Nations, the Australian Government and aid agencies. "They usually don't even try to use the law because they don't believe it will work and so resort to violence first."

But identifying the source of the moral corruption of an entire society is too sensitive and complicated a task. It may be legitimate to point to the so-called "warrior heritage" of traditional Khmer culture and the use of confrontation, rather than consensus, in the solving of disputes.

It would also be useful to recall that since 1970, when the Americans engineered a right-wing coup in Phnom Penh to suit their purposes in the war in neighbouring Vietnam, the Cambodian people have been trapped in a cycle of powerlessness, violence and corruption.

More specifically, the criminal violence in Phnom Penh may be linked to the low level of education among the present population. The Khmer Rouge reign in the capital from 1975 to 1978 forced the old educated elite out of the city to rural work-camps, where tens of thousands died or later fled across the border as refugees. The illiterate farmers who replaced the decimated educated class came to the capital from villages with no experience of the social structures of law and order.

On the Thai border 400,000 Cambodians lived in closed camps for up to 15 years until their repatriation under the UN-sponsored peace plan, beginning in 1992. By that time a whole new generation of Khmers had been born and raised, dependent on UN camp rations. For the camp people only the armed political factions fighting the war inside Cambodia or the black market border traders offered an alternative — the power which comes with carrying a gun — to the daily tedium of captivity.

Officially, the war in Cambodia is over according to the UN peace accord signed in Paris in 1991. Elections are due to be held later this month despite ongoing political violence, mainly on the part of the Khmer Rouge.

The camp people who have returned have been de-skilled by camp dependency. Many of the remaining Cambodian farmers have been pushed off their land by war. Tens of thousands of soldiers and civilians have been maimed by landmines and now beg for a living. Others have been demobilised, and then drifted into the urban centres without marketable skills — prime candidates for gang memberships.

The shift from a Soviet-style communist economy in the mid-1980s to the free market has created new problems of social envy alongside economic growth. Cambodians with money, often sent by relatives overseas, have grown rich from investment. Those with no access to funds have remained, literally, in the gutters. The powerless have-nots frequently seek to redress the injustice by gaining property through violence.

New money has also fuelled corruption at all levels of officialdom. It is virtually impossible, said one Phnom Penh resident, to achieve anything in Cambodia without paying a bribe.

The UN machine, with its new air-conditioned jeeps and 22,000 well-paid employees, has also come into criticism for distorting the local economy with its dollars, which have flooded the bars and brothels . . .

Sydney Morning Herald, 3 May, 1993, p. 10

THE UNITED STATES AND VIETNAM

Since the end of the war in Vietnam, the United States has been trying to erase the psychological effects of its defeat. In the Gulf War, President Bush clearly stated that the US-led 'victory' had at last laid to rest the stigma of the US defeat in Vietnam. He showed that he had learnt many lessons from Vietnam, one of which was to ensure that there was very strict control of the media. The attitude of the United States towards Vietnam today has been very clearly shaped by the loss of 50 000 US soldiers in Vietnam and the perception that the US was defeated. Its policy since could be seen as an attempt to punish Vietnam for its victory, to make sure that Vietnam remains a poor country, and to ensure that no other Asian countries are tempted to follow the Vietnamese example and oppose the US.

As part of the Paris Peace Agreement, the US was to provide $3 billion in aid to help rebuild Vietnam. So far, no aid has been given, and US opposition has also meant that World Bank development funds have been denied to Vietnam. There have been a succession of stages in the US refusal to help:

1975: The US condemned the invasion of South Vietnam by the North, and imposed a total trade and economic embargo.

1978: The US opposed the Vietnamese invasion of Cambodia, and made withdrawal from Cambodia the condition for ending the embargo.

1989: Vietnam withdrew from Cambodia. The US then demanded a full settlement of the issue of prisoners of war and those missing in action (POWs/MIAs) before it would lift the embargo.

DOCUMENT STUDY

US policy on relations with Vietnam

“It has been US policy since the early 1980's that normalization of relations with Vietnam can and should be considered only in connection with the Cambodian situation. Our position since then has been clear: normalization can occur only after a complete and verified withdrawal of Vietnamese troops from Cambodia in the context of an acceptable, comprehensive political settlement of the Cambodian conflict. The Vietnamese understand that the pace and scope of the development of a US-Vietnamese relationship will depend on their continued co-operation with us on the prisoner of war/missing in action (POW/MIA) issue and other humanitarian concerns.

The Department of State advises that the United States does not maintain diplomatic or consular relations with Vietnam. While US passports are valid for travel to Vietnam, the US Government ... discourages travel to Vietnam.

Unless authorized by the US Treasury Department, (financial) transactions with Vietnam or its nationals are prohibited.”

US Department of State, *Background Paper, Vietnam (1990)*

POWs/MIAs

> "While US senators probe Hanoi's archives for clues to 2500 missing US soldiers — a search that has delayed normalisation of relations with Vietnam — little effort has been made to open US archives which conceal clues to the fate of 200 000 Vietnamese soldiers missing in action in the Vietnam War.
>
> Yet those documents, and thousands more in Army archives and veterans' homes, could give Vietnamese families answers to the same questions that torment American families two decades after the war: where and how did their loved ones die?
>
> Writer Pham Tien Duat said, 'Vietnamese are very anxious to find out what happened to our missing soldiers, and we resent very much that the Americans search for their dead while we lack the money to do so.'... 'Knowing the burial place is important in the Confucian ethic. And the Taoists say the ghosts of the dead haunt the family without proper burial,' said Professor Pike...
>
> One US Army researcher said, 'The Vietnamese had a hard time understanding why the US wanted to send in archaeologists: they simply set up memorials in each province.' He cited one farmer who had lost two boys in the war and whose orchard was torn up in the search for American bones."

Ben Barber, The *Sunday Age*, 22 November, 1992, World section, p. 5

Discuss

- How are the personal and business dealings of Americans with Vietnam affected by the embargo?
- What would be the reaction of the Vietnamese to US actions over the POW/MIA issue? How might this affect US/Vietnamese relations when the embargo is lifted?

Important influences on US policy

Veterans: Vietnam veterans have been a vocal and influential lobby group in the US. They have been assisted by film and TV to the extent that 60 per cent of Americans still believe there are US prisoners in Vietnam.

Cambodian issue: Up to 1989, the US opposed Vietnam's intervention largely because it was backed by the Soviets. They went along with the Chinese line, and gave tacit support to the Khmer Rouge.

Dispensability: Vietnam, and Cambodia, are small countries that can easily be pushed aside in the US view of the world. Other issues, such as the Gulf War and the collapse of Communism in Europe and the Soviet Union, have taken precedence.

Business: US business interests are forced to sit back and watch other countries develop contacts with Vietnam. They want an end to the embargo.
Presidents: Presidents Reagan and Bush were both Republicans who took a very conservative line. It is likely that the approach of President Clinton will be different.

AUSTRALIA AND INDO CHINA

In the last few years particularly, Australia has developed very good relations with the governments of Vietnam, Laos and Cambodia. Australia also has a positive image amongst the people of these countries.

- Australia's role in the war in Vietnam was largely confined to one province. Many Vietnamese are not aware that Australia fought in Vietnam.
- Australia set up an embassy in Hanoi in 1973, before reunification, and has maintained solid diplomatic relations with the Vietnamese.
- Official aid to Vietnam was cut off in 1979, but has recently resumed. However, a lot of Australian aid has been provided to all of Indo China through Non-Government Organisations (NGOs) such as CARE, Freedom from Hunger and the Overseas Service Bureau.

There are other reasons for this positive image.

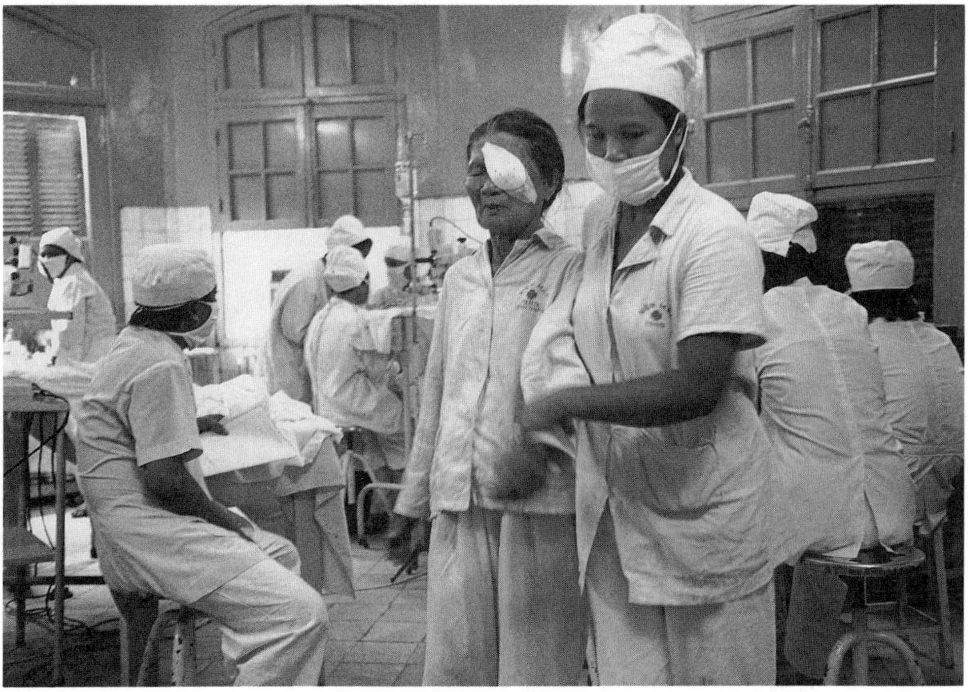

Australian Fred Hollows helped establish this eye clinic in Hanoi, to train Vietnamese doctors to treat eye diseases, particularly trachoma (courtesy Rob Elliott)

- Australia is seen as leading the way in the search for a diplomatic settlement in Cambodia. Our foreign policy is viewed as independent from the United States.
- Many Australian companies have set up in Vietnam, and their presence is visible. Our Overseas Telecommunications Service (OTC) has been active in providing communications in Vietnam and Cambodia.
- Australia has accepted 160 000 Indo-Chinese migrants. They have kept up contact with their relations and friends, and many are now returning for a visit. Travel is easier, and direct flights are available to Ho Chi Minh City.
- Individual Australians, such as Fred Hollows, have carried out valuable humanitarian work.
- Australia is building a bridge across the Mekong River near Vientiane. This $30 million bridge is being built by an Australian company, using Australian materials, and is funded by the Australian Government. This vital river crossing will link Laos and Thailand by road, and eventually road travel will be possible through to Vietnam and China.

Discuss

The following article looks at ways in which Indo-Chinese refugees have contributed to Australian society. Read the article carefully.

- What are the main ways in which the refugees have enriched the Australian way of life?
- What are the accusations that Sheridan says some people in Australia have made against the refugees? How does he answer the accusations?
- In what ways are the Vietnamese refugees 'now indelibly a part of the Australian character'?

From refugee to successful citizen... the Vietnamese have made a rapid transition, enhancing our culture and our development along the way

Refugees enrich doubting society

By foreign editor GREG SHERIDAN

WHEN Malcolm Fraser decided in the late 1970s that Australia would take in large numbers of Indo-Chinese boat-people it was primarily for reasons of pragmatic self-interest.

More than 1½ million Vietnamese were eventually to leave their homeland as refugees. This was partly in response to a crazy, anti-ethnic Chinese purge by the Hanoi authorities and partly in response to a generalised system of repression which the new communist rulers implemented in the old South Vietnam after their victory on April 30, 1975.

This vast human exodus put the main first asylum countries of the region, Malaysia, Thailand, Hong Kong, Indonesia and the Philippines, under immense pressure.

The United States, under a profound historical obligation to the Vietnamese refugees, brokered an international deal under which these countries offered first asylum to the boat people in exchange for an international resettlement program led by the US and involving, eventually, most of its allies.

Australia was under a triple pressure. We had participated fully in the Vietnam war and thus bore some responsibility for the events which led to the refugee crisis.

Most important of all perhaps, we were the most affluent country in the South-East Asian region. If we would not accept these refugees, the reason would be obvious.

And so with considerable trepidation, but also with considerable courage, Mr Fraser embarked on a refugee resettlement program which would earn us great credit internationally, but which would also profoundly change Australia.

Eventually we took more than 160,000 Indo-Chinese, more than 130,000 as refugees and 30,000 Vietnamese under the Orderly Departure Program. Of the 160,000 the overwhelming majority were Vietnamese.

On a per capita basis Australia took more Indo-Chinese refugees than any other nation in the world. It was the beginning of a new era for Australia.

The White Australia policy had been formally dead since the early 70s. But it was not until the advent of the boat people that we began to take large numbers of Asian immigrants.

The boat people were the forerunners of the more obviously economically beneficial Asian immigrants who were to play such a prominent part in the immigration program throughout the 80s and beyond.

The Vietnamese were to make an astonishingly rapid transition into the middle class and to make their contribution, especially in small business and, through their children, academically, with great speed.

The American neo-conservative, George Gilder, has argued that the US really won the Vietnam war. In the information age when knowledge is power, it won the only thing worth winning from Vietnam, a million industrious people profoundly committed to the values of family, industry and education.

Last year a Vietnamese refugee, Hung Ta, topped the NSW Higher School Certificate, a truly astonishing achievement for a young man who came to Australia as one of the boat people in 1979, aged five and fleeing the communists.

Hung's father is a factory worker and the family lives in the working class migrant suburb of Marrickville, in Sydney's inner-west.

He was a scholarship boy at Sydney Grammar, one of Sydney's top private schools.

The Vietnamese culture is a remarkably rich mixture of Chinese, Buddhist and Catholic influences. Its traditional, pre-colonial form of government emphasised a Chinese-style mandarinate class of advisers and governors.

The key to entering the mandarin class was scholarly excellence. At every level throughout traditional Vietnamese culture, education and scholarship have been emphasised.

It is a cultural norm which the refugees have brought with them to Australia.

The Vietnamese have been subject to some racism and negative stereotyping in Australia. One such is the fault of the media, sensationalising and "ethnicising" crimes committed by Vietnamese Australians.

Yet the statistics show that the crime rate for Vietnamese migrants is about one-third that of native-born Australians.

At times they have been accused of creating ghettos. Yet the facts show that their rate of out-settlement — that is, the speed with which they move out of the cluster suburbs in which they first settle and which are normally next to the migrant hostels in which they were originally accommodated — is actually greater than that of previous migrant groups.

Suburbs known for their Vietnamese population concentrations and shopping centres, such as Cabramatta in Sydney, are the reverse of ghettos.

They are populated by many non-Vietnamese (in fact, Vietnamese are nothing like a majority in Cabramatta), real estate prices in these suburbs have typically risen as a result of Vietnamese interest in them, and the shopping centres retain their distinctive ethnic flavour partly because tens of thousands of non-Vietnamese Australians like to go there to shop and eat at the restaurants and absorb the general feeling of the place.

The Minister for Foreign Affairs, Senator Evans, last year acknowledged on SBS Television that too many in the Labor Party had been slow to acknowledge the contribution of the Vietnamese because of previous ideological views on the Vietnam war.

But he personally, he said, had "great respect and admiration" for the refugees.

He went on to say that they had added a new dimension to Australian life and had been an important part of the development of Australian policy towards the region.

The senator is right. The Vietnamese *have* added a new dimension.

From their fabulous cuisine to the achievements of their children at school, from the unsurpassed heroism of many of their escape stories to the new patterns of Buddhist and Catholic religious observance flowering in the western suburbs of Sydney and Melbourne, from their love of family to the unfashionable continuing addiction of their men to cigarettes, they are now indelibly a part of the Australian character.

And we are much the richer for it.

Greg Sheridan, The *Australian*, 26 June, 1992, p. 13

NOTES

Chapter 1

1 Graham Walker in Kenneth Maddock & Barry Wright (eds), *War: Australia and Vietnam*, Harper & Row, Sydney, 1987, p. 11.
2 *As the Mirror Burns*, Musical Films, Melbourne, 1990, looks closely at the issue of birth defects.

Chapter 3

1 Stanley Karnow, *Vietnam: A History*, Penguin, Harmondsworth, 1986, p. 151.
2 David Halberstam, *Ho*, Barrie & Jenkins, London, 1971, p. 83.
3 Ibid., p. 91.

Chapter 4

1 Bernard Fall, *Vietnam Witness*, p. 8.
2 Robert Shaplen, *The Lost Revolution: Vietnam 1945–1965*, Andre Deutsch, London, 1966, p. 69.
3 Karnow, pp. 194–5.

Chapter 5

1 Gabriel Kolko,*Vietnam: Anatomy of War 1940–1975*, Unwin, London, 1987, p. 95.
2 Shaplen, p. 141.

Chapter 6

1 Karnow p. 386.

Chapter 7

1 Maddock & Wright, p. 11.
2 John Rowe,*Vietnam: The Australian Experience*, Time-Life, Sydney, 1987. Chapter 2 has an excellent account of the operation of the 1st Battalion.
3 I. M. Williams, *Vietnam: A Pictorial History of the Sixth Battalion, The Royal Australian Regiment*, Printcraft Press, 1967, p. 47.
4 Hugh Lunn, *Vietnam: A Reporter's War*, UQP, Brisbane, 1986, p. 142.
5 Terry Burstall, *A Soldier Returns*, UQP, Brisbane, 1990, p. 179.

Chapter 8

1 Robert B. Asprey,*War in the Shadows*, Macdonald & Janes, London, 1975, pp. 1297–8.
2 Kolko, p. 253.
3 Michael Maclear, *Vietnam: The Ten Thousand Day War*, Methuen, London, 1982, p. 203.
4 Asprey, pp. 1305–7.
5 Kolko, p. 260.

Chapter 9

1 Jeremy Barnes, *The Pictorial History of the Vietnam War*, Bison Books, London, 1988, p. 136.
2 Karnow, p. 546.
3 Maclear, p. 385.
4 Further information on the My Lai massacre is available in *The Australian Magazine*, 3–4 July 1989.

Chapter 10

1 *Sydney Morning Herald*, 15 April 1966.
2 Peter King (ed), *Australia's Vietnam*, Allen & Unwin, Sydney, 1983, p. 108.
3 Article by Malcolm Saunders.
4 Michael E. Hamel-Green in King, p. 113.
5 King, p. 208.
6 Ibid., pp. 112–13.
7 Maclear, p. 313. This is from his excellent chapter 'Front Line America'.
8 Lewis Chester, G. Hodgman & B. Page, *An American Melodrama: The Presidential Campaign of 1968*, Andre Deutsch, London, 1969, p. 5.
9 Karnow, p. 448.
10 Hugh Higgins, *Vietnam*, Heinemann, London, 1975, p. 100.
11 Karnow, p. 577.

Chapter 11

1 Higgins, p. 108.
2 Kolko, p. 371.
3 Barnes, p. 150.
4 Karnow, p. 602.
5 Kolko, p. 389.
6 Maclear, p. 126.
7 Karnow, p. 694.

Chapter 12

1 Described very well in Someth May, *Cambodian Witness*, Faber & Faber, London, 1988, pp. 86–7.
2 *The Killing Fields: The Facts behind the Film*, Coronet, London, 1984, p. 86.
3 May, especially pp. 139, 145, 168.
4 *Kampuchea*, a film by James Gerrand Productions, Australian Film Commission, 1988.
5 *Kampuchea*.
6 Gary Klintworth, 'Vietnam in Cambodia', *Current Affairs Bulletin*, September 1989, p. 22.
7 Quoted in Klintworth, p. 25.

BIBLIOGRAPHY

Asprey, Robert. *War in the Shadows*. Macdonald & Janes, London, 1975.

Baker, Mark. *Nam*. Sphere Books, London, 1982.

Barnes, Jeremy. *The Pictorial History of the Vietnam War*. Bison Books, London,1988.

Bennoun, Phillip, Bennoun, Robert & Kelly, Paula. *The Peoples from Indo-China*. Hodja Educational Resources Cooperative, Melbourne, 1984.

Bowden, Tim. *One Crowded Hour*. Collins, Sydney, 1987.

Burstall, Terry. *The Soldiers' Story*, UQP, Brisbane, 1987.

—— *A Soldier Returns*, UQP, Brisbane, 1990.

Buttinger, Joseph. *Vietnam: A Dragon Embattled*. Phaidon Press, 1967.

Chanoff, David & Toai, Doan Van. *Portrait of the Enemy*. I.B. Tauris, London,1986.

Chester, Lewis, Hodgson, Geoffrey & Page, Bruce. *An American Melodrama: The Presidential Campaign of 1968*. Andre Deutsch, London, 1969.

Fall, Bernard. *Street without Joy*. Schocken, New York, 1972.

—— *The Two Viet Nams: A Political and Military Analysis*. Frederick A. Praeger, New York, 1967.

Frost, Frank. *Australia's War in Vietnam*. Allen & Unwin, Sydney, 1983.

Halberstam, David. *Ho*. Barrie & Jenkins, London, 1971.

Herr, Michael. *Despatches*. Pan, London, 1981.

Higgins, Hugh. *Vietnam*. Heinemann, London, 1975.

Karnow, Stanley. *Vietnam: A History*. Penguin, Harmondsworth, 1986.

The Killing Fields: The Facts behind the Film. Coronet, London, 1984.

King, Peter (ed). *Australia's Vietnam*. Allen & Unwin, Sydney, 1983.

Kolko, Gabriel.*Vietnam: Anatomy of War 1940–1975*. Unwin, London, 1987.

Loewald, Uyen. *Child of Vietnam*. Hyland House, Melbourne, 1987.

Lunn, Hugh. *Vietnam: A Reporter's War*. UQP, St Lucia, 1986.

Maclear, Michael. *Vietnam: The Ten Thousand Day War*. Methuen, 1982.

Maddock, Kenneth & Wright, Barry (eds). *War: Australia and Vietnam*. Harper & Row, Sydney, 1987.

Mailer, Norman. *Miami and the Siege of Chicago*. Penguin, 1968.

May, Someth. *Cambodian Witness*. Faber & Faber, London, 1988.

McAulay, Lex. *The Battle of Long Tan*. Arrow, London, 1987.

Osborne, Milton. *Before Kampuchea: Preludes to Tragedy*. Allen & Unwin, Sydney, 1979.

Pilger, John. *Heroes*. Pan, London, 1986.

Rintoul, Stuart. *Ashes of Vietnam*. Heinemann, Melbourne, 1987.

Rowe, John. *Vietnam: The Australian Experience*. Time-Life, Sydney, 1987.

Sexton, Michael. *War for the Asking*. Penguin, Melbourne, 1981.

Shaplen, Robert. *The Lost Revolution: Vietnam 1945–1965*. Andre Deutsch, London, 1966.

Tuchman, Barbara. *The March of Folly*. Michael Joseph, London, 1984.

Truong Nhu Tang with Chanoff, D. and Toai, Doan Van. *A Vietcong Memoir*. Harcourt, Brace, Jovanovich, New York, 1985.

Vietnam: A Reporter's War. ABC, Sydney, 1975.

Williams, I.M. (Captain). *Vietnam: A Pictorial History of the Sixth Battalion, The Royal Australian Regiment*. Printcraft Press, 1967.

ACKNOWLEDGEMENTS

The author and publisher would like to acknowledge the following for permission to reprint copyright material: Abacus, pp. 96, 97; Allen & Unwin, pp. 74, 88, 89, 122; Alternative Publishing Co-operative, pp. 154, 156; Andre Deutsch, pp. 37, 54, 60, 64, 128; Arrow, p. 95; *Asiaweek*, p. 177; *The Australian*/Greg Sheridan, p. 187; *Backgrounder*, p. 164; Barrie & Jenkins, pp. 25, 26, 39, 43, 93; Bison Books, p. 69; *Border Mail*, pp. 9, 77, 125; *The Canberra Times*, p. 13; Collins, pp. 88, 142, 143, 152, 154; *Current Affairs Bulletin*, p. 162; Department of State Bulletin, p. 70; Department of State Publication, pp. 71, 72; Faber & Faber, p. 156; *Frederick A. Praeger*, p. 26; Greg Lockart, p., 42; Harcourt Brace Jovanovich, pp. 108, 145; Harper & Row, pp. 18, 69, 87; Hearings before Senate Sub-committee, p. 99; Heinemann, pp. 81, 125, 126; Ho Chi Minh, pp. 32, 35, 41, 43; P. J. Honey, p. 21; I. B. Tauris, p. 105; Macdonald & Janes, pp. 24, 56, 101; The Macquarie University Conference, pp. 7, 8; Methuen, pp. 94, 103, 116, 171; Michael Joseph, p. 126; National Library of Australia, pp. 14, 146, 147, 148; *New York Times*/Sydney H. Schanberg, p. 155; *New York Times* Syndication/Tiziano Terzani, p. 166; Pan, p. 142; Penguin, pp. 27, 48, 52, 75, 76, 77, 128; Phaidon Press, p. 25; Phongsavan Family, p. 172; Picador, p. 97; Printcraft Press, pp. 80, 83; Schocken, p. 44; *The Sunday Age*/Ben Barber, p. 184; *Sydney Morning Herald*, p. 167; *Sydney Morning Herald*/Lindsay Murdoch, pp. 181, 182; *Sydney Morning Herald*/Louise Williams, p. 182; *Time Australia Magazine*, pp. 14, 15; Time-Life, p. 89; Truong-Chinh, p. 43; Turnpike Press, pp. 117, 118; University of Queensland Press, pp. 88, 90, 92; Unwin, pp. 42, 45, 65, 104; US Department of State Bureau of Public Affairs, pp. 60, 61; US Department of State, p.183; *Vietnam-Courier; Information and Documents* p.71.

The author and publisher would also like to acknowledge permission to reproduce the following photographs and illustrations: *The Age*, p. 153; Australian Associated Press, p. 116 (right); Australian War Memorial, pp. 57, 79, Neg. No. DNE/65/428/VN, p. 82, Neg. No. GIL/67/483/VN, p. 83, Neg. No. BUL/69/27/VN, p. 84, Neg. No. CRO/68/575/VN, p. 85, FAI/70/223/VN, p. 91, Neg. No. CUN/66/521/VN; Bernard Martell, p. 127; Black Star, p. 49; *Border Mail*, p. 17; Tim Bowden & Neil Davis, courtesy Collins/Angus & Robertson, p. 144; Les Tanner/*Bulletin*, p. 75; John A. Ogle, p. 124; John Holland Group, p. 174; Magnum & Marc Riboud, pp. 103, 104; Mark Hall, p. 170; *Miami News*/Don Wright, p. 145; Michigan State University Archives and Historical Collections, p. 55; Mirror Australian Telegraph Publications, p. 122; Paris-Match, p. 48; Patti Collection, p. 32; Bruce Petty/*The Australian*, p. 138; Phongsavan Family, p. 173; Popperfoto, pp. 51 (right), 151; Rob Elliott Freelance Photography, pp. 10, 12, 157, 161, 163, 185; *Sydney Morning Herald*, p. 167; Saigon-Fall of Palace by Buffon-Darquenne/Sygma, p. 143; The Time-Life Inc. Company/Howard Sochurek, p. 54/Ronald Haeberle, p. 116 (left); UPI/Bettmann Newsphotos, pp. 59, 67, 132; UPI/K. Sawada, p. 102, & Van Es, p. 142; US Defense Department, pp. 27, 51 (left), 113; Wide World Photos, pp. 38, 112. All other photographs taken by the author.

Every attempt has been made to trace and acknowledge copyright holders. The publisher apologises for any accidental infringement and welcomes information that would redress the situation.

INDEX